Right-Wing Ireland?

Pressure Points in Irish Society

GENERAL SERIES EDITOR:
Professor Malcolm MacLachlan
Department of Psychology,
Trinity College Dublin

TITLES IN THE SERIES:

Cultivating Suicide? Destruction of Self in a Changing Ireland
by Caroline Smyth, Malcolm MacLachlan and Anthony Clare
(ISBN 1-904148-15-8)

The Politics of Drugs: From Production to Consumption
by Peadar King (ISBN 1-904148-19-0)

Right-Wing Ireland? The Rise of Populism
in Ireland and Europe
by Michael O'Connell (ISBN 1-904148-34-4)

FORTHCOMING TITLES:

Refuge in Ireland: Myth and Reality
by Treasa Galvin

Right-Wing Ireland?

The Rise of Populism in Ireland and Europe

Michael O'Connell

The Liffey Press

Published by
The Liffey Press Ltd
Ashbrook House, 10 Main Street
Raheny, Dublin 5, Ireland
www.theliffeypress.com

A catalogue record of this book is
available from the British Library.

ISBN 1-904148-34-4

Printed in the Republic of Ireland by Colour Books Ltd.

CONTENTS

ABOUT THE AUTHOR

Dr Michael O'Connell is a lecturer in social psychology at University College Dublin. His research interests are in the areas of inter-group relations, media representations, crime and social deprivation. He has published papers in leading journals; is co-editor of two books, *Crime and Poverty in Ireland* (Round Hall, Sweet and Maxwell, 1998) and *Cultivating Pluralism* (Oak Tree Press, 2000); and is the author of *Changed Utterly: Ireland and the New Irish Psyche* (The Liffey Press, 2001).

ACKNOWLEDGEMENTS

I wish to thank the following people for advice and help received in writing this book: Ciarán Benson, Diana Caffrey, Caroline Corr, John Garry, Pauline Grace, Alastair Green, Fiachra Kennedy, Michael Marsh, James McBride, Barbara Mennell, Ian O'Donnell, Michael O'Toole, Diana Payne, Richard Sinnott and Nessa Winston. Of course, all errors in fact and argumentation remain my sole responsibility. Professor Malcolm MacLachlan provided the initial encouragement to consider writing this book as well as early feedback on ideas about its structure.

The book would not have appeared without the professionalism and sharp instincts of David Givens and Brian Langan at The Liffey Press.

Series Introduction

The *Pressure Points in Irish Society* series presents concise critical commentaries on social issues of contemporary concern. These books are written to be accessible, topical and, if necessary, controversial. Their aim is to "add value" to social debate by highlighting neglected issues, developing new perspectives on an existing debate or presenting new data that can enlighten our thinking. Each of the topics addressed in the series in some sense challenges complacency, upsets a sense of social equilibrium or questions the status quo. In short, *Pressure Points* is concerned with those issues that suggest "everything is not OK".

The term "pressure point" can of course mean different things in different contexts. One meaning of a "pressure point" is an issue that can be targeted by political pressure or influence. However, for many important social issues, political pressure is often not mounted by those within the political establishment, but rather by specific pressure groups, non-governmental organisations, community actions or campaigning individuals. The reluctance of many politicians to "make an issue" out of problems such as drugs, suicide, disability or immigration — to name but a few — is probably because they see them as quagmires from which there is no easy exit; or perhaps more cogently, no easy "exit poll" for their political savvy to weigh up. Many of our most destructive social issues are quite simply not vote winners. In the sense of applying pressure in the body politic, then, *Pressure Points* hopes to highlight issues that have been insufficiently debated, or considered in a blinkered fashion.

Another meaning of "pressure point", in the "body physical", as it were, is a place on the body where an artery can be pressed against a bone in order to stop bleeding. This calls forth the spectre of a system haemorrhaging and needing acute intervention. Here, there is not only a sense of immediacy, but also of weakness in one system threatening the viability of the whole body. Systems theory, of course, conceptualises problems not as singular entities but as interconnected and mutually reinforcing or diminishing phenomenon. Such thinking is central to the practice of social sciences: problems need to be considered in a broad societal context, rather than being seen as discrete entities in isolated systems working away on their own.

While the Chinese wish "may you live in interesting times", we in Ireland certainly do. The advent of the so-called "Celtic Tiger" brought us economic prosperity undreamt of a mere decade earlier. The uneasy "Peace Process" has arrested the relentless and senseless demeaning of an island soaked in the blood of its intolerance. The hitherto unanticipated net migration into Ireland has transformed our image of an island to "leave from", to one of an island to "arrive at". This has presented us with new challenges and opportunities, not least the opportunity to see our own cultural conflict in a much broader perspective. As such, the call for pluralism in Ireland not only offers a warmer and more considered welcome to immigrants, but also a warmer and more considered welcome to the "others" within our island.

Alongside economic prosperity and the peace process, we have also experienced a decline in the iconography of traditionally significant social figures. Priests, doctors, politicians and other stalwarts of the social order have, at least as collective entities, fallen from a presumption of benevolence, propriety and public service. Some of our priests have abused the trust of a nation and raped the innocence of our children; many doctors (and others) extort fees for private consultations and in so doing further undermine the public services they are handsomely paid to provide; while some politicians have been found to be up to their necks in corruption. Such events have profoundly affected the presumption of living in a pro-social "civil" society. Collective identity and the fear of God have giving way to individuation and the fear of negative equity, in lives now mortgaged to the hilt. Economic success has congested our cities, recast our social values and provided a materialistic common denominator into which our "value" is being weighed up.

It is the nature of any rapidly changing society that while some social virtues are lost, others are gained. People now feel they

have greater civil liberties, greater access to the previously secret workings of the state, freedom to divorce, freedom to cohabit
and have children out of wedlock and recently (and perhaps most
dramatically), freedom to demonstrate their overwhelming wish
that our government not facilitate war. Ultimately, it is not change
per se that is good or bad, right or wrong, moral or immoral, but
how we adapt to our new circumstances. It has always been the
"job" of culture to make the lives of its members meaningful and
to offer them guidelines for living — feeling valued and having a
place in the world. The reach of globalisation, with its myriad
mechanisms, such as the internet, television, and retail outlets,
presents us afresh with the perennial challenge of deciding what
we are about. Yet this need for identity, for rootedness, occurs in
a completely new global context, with new "free trade" masters
in a world pulsating to corporate interests, in an enlarged European Union in which we will inevitably have less influence.

How we respond to the pressure points in Irish society will de-
fine who we are and what factors are most influential over us.
While a concern over how a small island like Ireland responds to
global challenges may seem to be rather a parochial concern, in
fact it is not. The world is made up of small communities with ethnic, religious and sometimes national identities. How local systems interact with global systems is of worldwide interest, as is
captured by that ugly term "globalisation". Our concerns in Ireland may well be particular, but how we adapt to global issues is
of general interest and importance. Many of the titles in this series
arise from the local presentation of issues of global import.

I am very pleased to be associated with The Liffey Press's
series on *Pressure Points in Irish Society*. We hope that in a modest way these books will advance thinking and practice in their
target areas and that you will enjoy reading them and be enli-
vened by them. Finally, I invite all interested parties, from all
walks of life, who have the drive to tackle such issues in a critical and concise manner, to join us by submitting a proposal to
myself or The Liffey Press, for a future book in this series.

Malcolm MacLachlan,
Department of Psychology,
Trinity College Dublin.

This book is dedicated with love and thanks to Pauline

Chapter 1

THE CHANGING FACE(S) OF IRELAND

Like other forces of globalisation, immigration is disruptive, and at the most intimate level. It changes the neighbourhood. People in the street speak odd languages; the neighbours' cooking smells strange. So immigration often meets passionate resistance. Even in countries built on immigration, like the United States, politicians hesitate to press for easier entry . . . In Europe, hostility is deeper and can be more dangerous . . . The hostility may well increase . . . If the economic slowdown persists, unemployment is sure to breed greater resentment. (*The Economist*, 2 November 2002, p. 11)

The Government has accepted that voters are "disappointed" with the economic downturn, but denied again that it had conned them before the election . . . [The Taoiseach] said: "People feel a little disappointed that it's not as good as it was. They'd like to be back to where it was and so would we." (*The Irish Times*, 4 June 2003)

[Professor Kader Asmal] said yesterday he was appalled at the "apparent racism, discrimination and xenophobia which had taken root in Irish society" (*The Irish Times*, 30 August, 2003)

The above quotes capture the new sombre mood of our time; long gone the exuberant confidence of the nineties. It's back to basics in the world of politics — votes, jobs, economic slowdown and immigration. In Ireland, where for so long business has been anything but usual, these concerns are now being expressed. The second leg of a referendum on Europe saw both sides using the issue of jobs or rather joblessness as their main

campaign threat. And although one would never have guessed
it from the surreal rhetoric of the 2002 general election, the
economic slowdown has been patently obvious from the middle
of 2001 to everyone (bar possibly the economists whose job it is
to observe these things). And immigration? Yes, it too has become a concern, if not yet an always openly expressed one, for
large sections of the Irish public. As Stephen Collins, political
editor of the *Sunday Tribune*, noted:

> Immigration is now a major issue lurking below the surface
> of political debate . . . Focus group research carried out by
> Fianna Fáil and Fine Gael before the last election showed
> that immigration was an issue with a significant proportion
> of the electorate. (*Sunday Tribune*, 27 October 2002, p. 12)

"Concerns about immigration" frequently translates into anti-
immigration feeling which of course regularly overlaps with
racism. Racism in Ireland has become an important political issue. This represents an important change. Irish racists in the
past were a curiosity; like hermits with a great sense of humour,
there were probably lots of them out there. It was, however,
difficult to identify them unless and until they emigrated to a
multicultural society when their attitudes became manifest. (Of
course, this is only true if one overlooks the virtually routine
and virulent hostility of many settled Irish people towards Travellers.) But now, as we shall see, a transformed Ireland provides a much larger set of worries and targets for the racist
and/or the anti-immigrationist. This is a real turn-around; in the
past, we were accustomed to our role as honourable victims of
racism. Important research for example was carried out in de-
tecting the anti-Irish prejudice "deeply embedded in English
culture" (Curtis, 1984). Now, the sharp sociological scrutiny
must turn inwards as the Irish become both subject and object
in the study of racism. Or as McVeigh and Lentin put it, "Ireland
is quintessentially 'between two worlds' — both perpetrator
and survivor of racism, both thoroughly racist and deter-
minedly anti-racist" (p. 8).

In attitudes to Europe too, a change has occurred. Euro-
scepticism, previously a rare and exotic species in the Irish
ecosystem, is edging its way into the political mainstream.

There are of course perfectly rational reasons for being scepti-
cal about the European project. It may not be *communautaire*
but it is certainly sensible to question the direction and pace of
EU evolution. But that is not at all the same thing as Euro-
scepticism and its knee-jerk hostility to all things European-
related. That current has had no force of substance in Irish society until very recently. Thus we are witnessing (and further
evidence will be provided for this below) the apparent rise of
both anti-immigrationism and Euro-scepticism as serious play-
ers in the Irish political system. At one level, this is unremarkable; these views are widespread in most EU countries and
elsewhere. But at another level, the transformation of Irish politics and the consolidation of these two sets of views, opposition
to Europe and opposition to immigration, these bridgeheads of
the European New Right, is extraordinary, given how quickly
they have occurred. The speed of these changes, their current
potency as well as their likely scope need to be assessed and
their implications weighed up.

The case will be argued that Irish conservatism is shifting —
indeed has shifted — from a traditional Catholic clericalism to a
radical right-wing populism. The characteristics of this populism are spelled out in greater detail in Chapter Three but for
those readers who require a greater degree of clarity at this
point, one must summarise the components of this new form of
politics as (a) radical, in that its advocates often reject important
elements of consensus politics; (b) right-wing, in that it includes
a component of hostility to foreigners or outsiders; and (c)
populist, in that its rhetoric seeks to exploit an alleged chasm
between an unrepresentative political elite and an unrepre-
sented general public.

THE NEW ECONOMIC AND POLITICAL LANDSCAPE

The most obvious element of change in Irish society for many
since the mid 1990s was related to the economy. The "basket
case" of the eighties turned top of the class in the nineties with
extraordinary economic growth being registered. Close to
double-digit GDP and GNP figures were recorded over the
mid- to late nineties. Such was the sustained nature of economic

growth that Ireland entered the new millennium as one of the
wealthiest nations in the EU and by corollary the world. The
growth rates recorded in the year 2000, for example, were re-
markable: a GDP increase of 10.1 per cent and a GNP increase
of 10.2 per cent (at constant 1995 prices) (Department of Finance, *Monthly Economic Bulletin*, August 2003). Spectacular
and ongoing growth meant that the traditional, chronic and
apparently more or less permanent problems of under-
investment, unemployment and mass emigration were actually
resolved, at least temporarily. The emigration boat and plane
were unknown to a new generation of young Irish citizens. And
it felt good to think, even though it only lasted so briefly, that
the government actually had money to throw at problems in areas like education, infrastructure and health.

But as is the way of these things, success has thrown up a
few problems of its own. An ESRI publication (Layte et al.,
2001), based on a longitudinal wave of surveys, found that Ireland became a far more inegalitarian society between 1994 and
1998. The haves, both through the policies of a highly ideological government, and as a by-product of rapid growth, have become relatively far better off as a result of the boom of the
nineties. The periods of sharpest increases in general growth
coincide with the years of widening disparity between the poor
and rich. The important but ultimately modest increases in the
absolute income of those relying on social welfare or in poorly
paid jobs could not match the comparatively massive windfalls
generated by tax reductions among the better off (and were
largely wiped out by inflation anyway). So Ireland has become
a far wealthier society and at the same time (and partly as a
consequence), a far less equal society. We will see later that
inequality and attitudes towards immigrants are strongly intertwined. The effect of *relative deprivation* independent of *absolute deprivation* is considered in subsequent chapters.

Furthermore, strange and worrying things happened to
house prices. Bijou urban dwellings rocketed in nominal value.
Even the notion of a "family homestead" became meaningless
for many. That is not to say that people did not still yearn to own
a house in a traditionally good or local area but aspiration and
ability were no longer even closely aligned. Housing is a funda-

mental and therefore emotional issue for most; the economic tornado of the nineties picked many people from where they hoped or wanted to live and flung them aside, into new regions, often sociologically disjointed commuter villages, further undercutting the traditional social fabric. In fact, it is difficult to underestimate the role of housing in shaping, literally as well as attitudinally, contemporary Irish society. The frothy increases in prices is reminiscent of the boom years in the UK under Thatcher; the subsequent era of negative equity and housing crises that ultimately did for Thatcher hang over all purchasers of high-priced accommodation now. And creating even further waves of inequality, for some the property problem means finding somewhere to live while for others, it is the issue of what to buy to obtain the greatest return. Of course, these divergences are not completely novel but the disparities in the meaning and function of property for different sections of the population are ever more pronounced. And finally we will see, in subsequent chapters, how explosive an issue property becomes when minorities are involved; the older fear of losing value on one's house because of the proximity of a Travellers' halting site has long contributed an economic component to an already explosive prejudice. Now resentment over the perceived "cushiness" of accommodation provided for asylum-seekers has been added to the equation. Growing integration of European policy also lessens the instruments (such as interest rates) available to the national government to fine-tune factors like house-price growth.

The Catholic church has struggled to keep pace with the changes in people's lives. This is only to be expected; the rate of change has been so rapid and the terrain has altered so quickly that any large institution whose aim is to provide leadership and guidance over all aspects of people's lives would have found it a serious challenge. But what makes it especially hard is that in the late eighties, it looked like the church had succeeded in maintaining if not strengthening its grip on the population. In retrospect, many of the ferocious ideological battles at the time signalled the beginning of the end of church hegemony. Power, as Lukes (1974) has pointed out, is at its most sweeping when it is uncontested and so prevents people from seriously thinking about alternatives. Thus the referenda appearing to copper-

fasten Catholic ideology into Irish law in the eighties in fact revealed an awakening secular consciousness and the end of
Catholic supremacy. The endgame is still being played out but,
since the Robinson election and more especially the successful
divorce referendum of late 1995, the war is over and a liberal set
of values reigns. Religious belief, previously a contested domain,
is now one of private conscience. It is also increasingly a minority concern. Statements of the church hierarchy, once command-
ing universal attention and respect, now conjure up indifference
or occasionally vociferous criticism. Accusations that the church
shielded or even abetted serial child sex abusers by moving
them on whenever their activities were being exposed have put
the church hierarchy on the defensive. Ironically, the fading of
church power may aid the growth of a new populist right in a
number of ways. Firstly, as will be argued in greater detail below, its demise leaves a gap in the political market for an authoritarian ideology. Conservatives on the whole will seek a new way
to express their ideology. Secondly, for the declining number of
conservatives who do remain attached to a form of Christian fun-
damentalism, Euro-scepticism will be increasingly attractive;
Brussels and the EU are perceived as operating to a liberal anti-
family agenda. And finally, the Catholic church has actually been
positive in sending out a strong message about the needs of the
vulnerable in society and the dangers of anti-immigrant racism.
Its weakened position now is such that a call on people to do
their Christian duty in regard to minorities and the vulnerable is
unlikely to be widely heeded.

Despite the major battles across the religious–secular divide
as well as the fault-line of soft versus hard nationalism underpinning popular ideologies, the Irish political system has actually
remained remarkably constant. One may wish to follow the psy-
choanalytic distinction between manifest and latent; the manifest
refers to those things on the surface, while latent deals with the
deeper, less visible but usually more meaningful and influential
issues well below the surface. The intention of the author in subsequent chapters in fact may well be summarised as trying to get
at some of the latent elements, especially around public beliefs
and attitudes, shaping the future. And it is argued that this latent
material, "lurking below the surface of political debate"

(Stephen Collins, quoted earlier), is in rapid change. But certainly the manifest political landscape, the domain of the Dáil and the Seanad, the polity in a word, is recognisably similar in the first decade of this century as it was, say, in the 1960s and 1970s. The slow but inexorable decline of the two major parties continues. Their combined share of first preference votes at 64 per cent in 2002 compares to 82 per cent in 1981, 73.5 per cent in 1989 and is the lowest since the 62 per cent of 1948 (although their combined 1992 vote also registered at 64 per cent) (Sinnott, 1995). That Fine Gael's performance was disastrous is uncontroversial although its poor return in seats for votes cast exaggerated the general catastrophic perception. But Fianna Fáil is also in decline — its deep crisis is demonstrated by the fact that it turned in its third worst vote in the history of state general elections despite governing over an unprecedented economic boom. Its excellent vote management partly disguised the low vote. (It also appears to support Garret FitzGerald's contention that the party's core voters are an ageing demographic group.) The Labour Party continues to under-perform despite annexing the capable forces of Democratic Left; the weak Irish left of course makes it easier for right-wing forces to blossom. The election of 2002 also confirmed that small political parties are viable under Ireland's generous PR system and that the system is permeable both to ideological parties (the Greens and Sinn Féin) as well as to single-issue (e.g. health) candidates. These single-issue independents often liaise between the manifest and latent areas of politics (although a number of them in the 2002 election were disgruntled former Fianna Fáilers). A paradox is that we have a system that is fairly open to change and yet remains almost as stable as those in the UK or US. Some of our political stalwarts are fine parliamentary performers but most hang in there by capable clientelism. In other words, success for most politicians requires them to be very responsive to local and constituency concerns; they may not be able to do much about them in most cases but they have to make the right sounds. It will be argued that this makes it all the more likely that current under-the-surface or latent issues will push their way through into the national political scene. Anti-immigration resentment as well as Euro-scepticism are precisely these kinds of latent issues.

SLUMP POLITICS

It hardly needs reiteration but of course the assessments above are based on the social change emanating from a period of incredible growth in the Irish economy. The question that naturally arises is what happens when economic success unravels. Unfortunately, the lesson of national histories in the twentieth century is that if economic growth produces at least weak movement away from authoritarianism, inflexibility, parochialism and xenophobia, economic failure massively strengthens these forces across all social strata. In particular, those who had aspired to the better things but feel all is lost are most dangerous as the behaviour of the *petit bourgeoisie*, the "grocers" and little businessmen, have proven in many circumstances. There are few more reactionary forces than a million pissed-off yuppies who can't meet their mortgage repayments. And the brutal reality is that this is precisely the scenario of at least the short-term future. And short term is optimistic here; we have entered what looks like a world slump. To find comparable losses in share values in 2002, for example, one has to go back to the late 1920s.

In late 2003, some commentators have begun to make vaguely optimistic noises about turning around the world slump but it is difficult to see how this might happen. The once powerhouse that was the Japanese economy ambles to a halt under the festering sore of its unreformed banking sector (see *The Economist*, "The ghosts of reforms past", 31 October 2002). The Latin American economies offer no hope — Argentina has been shattered, Brazil faces huge poverty while Venezuela's government is under unremitting internal attack. Sub-Saharan Africa continues to worsen in real terms. Stagnation and recession in Germany have spread to France, Italy and the Netherlands. An increasingly bellicose US leadership exacerbates the problem in its transparent and single-minded objective of carving out and controlling world oil supplies; economists label its fragile recent recovery as jobless (i.e. failing to tackle the problem of unemployment) and many of its individual states like California teeter on the brink of bankruptcy and surreal political solutions.

We may wish to think in Ireland that this is all simply bad news about bad things happening elsewhere. But the much-vaunted openness of the Irish economy was not just IDA guff. Economic success was to a great extent contingent on world economic success, especially of US firms. To hope for a re-run of the 1990s in the next few years is absurd. How will an era of slump (or at best stagnation) impact on politics and popular morale? Ted Gurr, a political scientist, in his influential book *Why Men Rebel* (1970) argued that such situations, as demonstrated by many societies, and in different eras, were socially explosive. He suggested that an era of year-on-year success where a significant improvement in the standard of living became the norm led to a phenomenon of "aspirational deprivation" when the economy goes flat. Returns plateau out but the population has learned to expect much more — the current government or regime becomes massively discredited. It was formerly said of the left, particularly the revolutionary left, that it secretly welcomed the aspirational deprivation of the masses of this sort, to easier demonstrate the inability of market capitalism to produce a stable and steady amelioration of people's living conditions. Whatever the truth of this, all will concede that the revolutionary left is not ideally placed to benefit from the current slump; the collapse of the Soviet Union still casts a shadow over leftist thinking and internationalist and socialist ideology are weak. Classic social psychological models in fact argue that in the absence of an over-arching ideology, the likely consequence of a struggle over resources, of "realistic group conflict" will be increased hostility between social groups as well as scapegoating of weaker groups. In a world economic slump, where the perceived economic pie is fixed rather than growing, the struggle for resources is a zero-sum competition; if they benefit, it means I've lost and my gain will have to be at their expense. This zero-sum competition will impact on people's attitudes towards politics in Ireland in two ways:

- Externally, one can expect growing resentment of the applicant and new-member states in the EU, seen as supplanting Ireland's traditional role of net recipient of subsidies. Benign indifference to Europe will gradually be replaced by sharp hostility as Ireland is expected to accept its role as a modest net contributor to, rather than absorber of, EU funds.

- Internally perceived "sponges" on the economy will face greater animus from ever more substantial sections of society, especially those feeling their livelihoods are insecure. Asylum-seekers, ethnic minorities, immigrants and foreigners generally will be blamed for either not working and sponging off the state, or working and therefore taking jobs from Irish people.

In other words, it is predicted that the coming slowdown will bring forth previously latent tensions and concerns and these will likely be directed into Euro-scepticism and anti-immigrationist ideology. With a permeable political system available, it means that Ireland is ripe for the forces of the populist right.

THE EUROPEAN DEBATE

One of the most surprising political events of the recent Irish political past was the rejection of the first Nice Treaty. Constitutional law meant that an EU enlargement policy for ten new, mainly central European states was put to the Irish electorate for ratification rather than solely being decided by the government. Almost 54 per cent of voters in 2001 rejected the Treaty. The half-hearted debate in the first referendum focused heavily on the issue of militarisation, although this was probably a red herring and played a much smaller part in the second referendum. What lay behind this apparent ingratitude towards Europe, a Europe that has provided €32 billion to Ireland in 30 years, through agricultural and regional development subsidies (*Economist*, 19 October 2002, p. 35)? Was this a symptom of underlying Euro-scepticism or merely one of those odd political blips? What was in the mind of the Irish voter as he/she rejected the referendum? Certainly not Europe, suggest those who believe in the "blip" position. Only 34 per cent of people bothered to vote in the referendum, and many from both the left and right simply wished to give the ruling parties a bloody nose; thus the rejection was not in fact a vote against enlargement. Accordingly, when the major political parties mobilised properly and put time and money into the second referendum, it passed comfortably with almost 63 per cent in favour as Ireland's traditional Europhilia reappeared.

There is a problem with this perspective, though. The re-run of the referendum was hopelessly one-sided: the funds available to the "No" side were completely dwarfed by that of the "Yes"; the coalition of groups in favour of a "Yes" vote was very broad, ranging from the major political parties to business groups, trade unions, and farming organisations. Furthermore, the Greens, one of the more coherent forces opposed to the Nice Treaty, was badly split with its allies in the European parliament on the correct tactical approach to take. And yet . . . the vote was far from an overwhelming endorsement of the treaty. The abstention level was over 50 per cent, despite the pressure from the major social forces. An occasional paradox of voter apathy is that people sometimes have to care strongly enough about something not to vote on the issue. Individuals can work their way through the most esoteric literature and Byzantine arguments when they feel something important is at stake. The victory of the "Yes" side was premised on persuading enough people to believe that future prosperity and employment were at risk if the second referendum was lost. Despite these threats and heavy spending, however, the government and major political parties failed to persuade any more than about a third of voters that they should vote "Yes". The others voted "No" or (more commonly) weighed up the pros and cons and decided against voting. This is a clear case of Euro-scepticism, weak but growing, that is still in search of a political home.

Professor Brigid Laffan has argued that widespread penetration by British media has "infected the Irish with the virus of Euro-scepticism" (quoted in *The Economist*, 19 October 2002, p. 35) (and presumably infected the Irish media also). Whatever the validity of this argument, it is certainly true that all the classic concerns about the EU previously more common to conservative, populist and far-right parties in the UK and continental Europe rumbled on in the background of these referenda: the loss of power in an ever-larger Union; the perception of the threat of immigrants from applicant states as well as illegal immigrants (and especially those of ethnic minorities) from elsewhere; the feeling that national sovereignty was being eroded through the expansion in areas over which the EU claimed competence. The latter, national sovereignty, was something we were willing to concede as a luxury in the past in return for economic gain; now that economic existence was less precarious for most, greater numbers of voters felt the threat to national decision-making. The feeling that applicant states might usurp Ireland's traditional advantages within the EU (as a low corporate tax area and healthy recipient of aid) undoubtedly also played a role. In Chapter Two, the evidence behind the claim that Ireland is growing more Euro-sceptic will be examined in detail and the unmistakable trends in opinion, derived from large-scale representative surveys as well as elsewhere, will be presented.

CITIZENS AND VISITORS

Ireland's changing relationship to Europe is, however, secondary in comparison to the changing demography of the country over relatively short periods of time. Chronic and problematic features of Irish life — emigration and patterns of declining population growth — so evident especially in the middle decades of the last century, disappeared. In 1991, the census reported a national population of approximately 3,526,000. Five years later, this had increased to 3,626,000, an increase of about 100,000. However, by the following census of 2002,[1] the increase in population within a six-year period was almost 300,000 (291,249) with a population now registering 3,917,000. Analysis of the CSO figures demonstrates that some of this increase was "natural", i.e. it was caused by an increase of births over deaths. However this only accounts for 47 per cent or less than half of the increase. The rest of the increase was caused by net migration. This was one of the few intercensal periods showing positive rather than negative net migration (i.e. showing more people immigrating than emigrating) and is the only intercensal period where the estimated per annum net migration (25,511) exceeds the estimated per annum natural increase

---

[1] The census planned for April 2001 was postponed until April 2002 because of the threat of a foot-and-mouth epidemic.

(23,030). Ireland, unlike say France, has historically been a country of emigration and the recent phase of immigration has been a novel one, entirely unpredicted by any social observer.

In 2002, it is estimated that 18,800 people migrated from Ireland while 47,500 migrated into the country. CSO figures reveal that 36 per cent of immigrants were from either the UK or the US and it seems likely that many of these were Irish nationals returning to live in Ireland attracted by impressive economic growth rates. A further 18 per cent were from other EU countries and the remaining 46 per cent or 17,500 were described as coming from "rest of world". What distinguishes this period from the other time in recent years where net migration was positive (1971–79) was the diversity of some of the migrants. In the past, ethnic, national or religious diversity often came about largely through returning Irish migrants being accompanied by spouses of different backgrounds. In the 1990s, though, economic opportunities for immigrants on the one hand as well as humanitarian crises and wars in Africa and parts of Eastern Europe have led to a much broader range of people seeking to live in Ireland. Couples and families of different cultural origin are also likely to find it more difficult to integrate in comparison to ones where one partner is an "insider"(native Irish).

In 2001, 10,325 applications for asylum were received by the Office of the Refugee Applications Commissioner. The top six COIs (Countries of Origin) of the applicants in that year making up over 61 per cent of the applicants were Nigeria, Romania, Moldova, Ukraine, Russia and Croatia (Appendix 3, p. 65 of the Annual Report of the Office of the Refugee Applications Commissioner). Over a five-year period (1997–2001), there is a good deal of year-to-year consistency in the pattern reported. Figure 1.1 below presents information on the numbers seeking asylum from the four most common countries of origin during that period.

Figure 1.1: The Total Number of Asylum Applications from the Four Most Common "Countries of Origin" into Ireland, 1997–2001

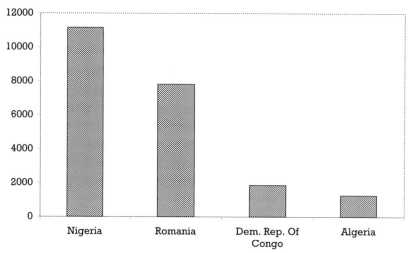

Source: UNHCR Statistical Yearbook, 2001, p. 120.

In that period, 41,421 asylum seekers from Algeria made first applications to any European country, as did 40,210 asylum-seekers from the Democratic Republic of Congo (DRC), 44,643 from Romania and 32,248 Nigerians (calculated from figures derived in Annex C.7 of the UNHCR Statistical Yearbook 2001). Thus, 3.0 per cent of Algerian asylum-seekers made their first applications to Ireland in that period, 4.6 per cent of those from the DRC, 17.5 per cent of Romanians and 34.6 per cent of Nigerian asylum-seekers. The situation for asylum-seekers from these four countries will be returned to in Chapter Five.

Aside from asylum-seekers, who are not allowed to work while their claim is being processed, 40,321 temporary (one-year) visas were also issued to applicants from non-EEA countries[2] in 2002. These employment visas are only provided where an employer finds no worker from Ireland or other EU countries available for a position (the test of unavailability is advertisement for a number of weeks by FÁS). The countries

---

[2] EEA: The European Economic Area consisting of the fifteen EU states as well as Norway, Iceland and Liechtenstein.

whose citizens have received the greatest numbers of temporary work visas have tended to be applicants for EU membership and the visa requirement will disappear from May 2004 for these people, assuming the Accession Treaties run to plan. In the first three months of 2003, for example, an analysis of work permits by nationality shows that the largest numbers went to Lithuania (958), Latvia (883), the Philippines (851) and Poland (801) of the 9,523 issued (source: www.entemp.ie/lfd/wp-janstats.htm).

The Economist (8 June 2002, p. 28) estimates, on the basis of OECD figures, that in the period 1996–2000, Ireland was ranked fourth of EU countries in total of asylum-seekers per 1,000 population. Belgium and Netherlands accepted substantially more and Austria marginally so. The report of the Office of the Refugee Applications Commissioner comments that Ireland has experienced a "phenomenal increase in asylum applicants in the past decade from 39 in 1992 to 1,179 in 1996 to 10,938 in 2000" (Appendix 1, p. 54). One should be wary of the word "phenomenal". Ireland's increase looks phenomenal mainly because the comparison point of people seeking asylum ten years ago was close to zero. Within the EU, Ireland's position on numbers of asylum-seekers is above average only because of the increasing hardening of borders by all EU countries. Net migration per annum represents merely 0.007 of the 2002 population overall. Only a very small proportion of asylum-seekers are offered refugee status (893 in 2002) and the population remains very homogeneous, especially in comparison to the post-imperial and so-called "traditional immigration" countries in the EU.

Nevertheless, for people living in urban areas in Ireland, the sense of palpable change cannot be denied; where once a dark-skinned face would have been a novelty, it is now unremarkable, especially in Dublin. Shops and restaurants catering to new ethnic groups have sprung up in a few places. And media reports and political commentary, not always sympathetic, dealing with new minorities have also appeared. In supermarket chains in Dublin, the norm is increasingly that one is served by a non-Irish shopping assistant. Previous interaction with minority groups by Irish people was generally restricted to travel abroad or indirectly via the media. The tiny number of people from different ethnic or cultural backgrounds in Ireland were likely to be students, often displaying a cosmopolitan ease shared by the international elite. But now with larger numbers of minority groups from varying class backgrounds in Ireland, interaction between "insider" and "outsider" is not restricted to the relatively relaxed world of third-level educational institutions. Rather, it is in the real, gritty everyday world that it occurs. And, of course, not being "posh" doesn't ease the potential hostility of the local populace; the diversity of prejudice is such that you can be resented for being privileged or under-privileged. If anything, and as occurred widely in the UK, the areas on which the greatest demands for integration are made are the tough, often deprived urban ones. Travelling through Dublin, for example, one is less likely to encounter racial diversity along the well-heeled DART villages like Howth and Sandymount; rather, it is in the north inner city, an area with a history of unremitting deprivation where one meets the new immigrants: the sad-eyed African man on Amiens Street, the chatty oriental couple on O'Connell Street, the exuberant African children in the Jervis Street Shopping Centre or the anxious Russian men on Capel Street.

The widely read tabloid, the *Sunday World* suggested that "New York has one, San Francisco has one, as do most European cities. Now Dublin has its own 'Little Africa'" (p. 2, special supplement, 22 September 2002), an area extending from Parnell Street to Gardiner Street into Moore Street and west towards Smithfield. The tone of the article — "from inside the city's vibrant new ethnic enclaves" — is a curious one, managing to be warm, patronising and threatened all at the same time. One senses that the tabloids still haven't quite finalised how to run with the whole minorities issue — plucky new entrepreneurs or criminal underclass, it's up for negotiation. This article is mainly positive and it highlights that a number of businesses — bars, Internet cafés, supermarkets and hair salons — catering for African immigrants have developed in "one of Dublin's most historical and traditional areas". With some tabloid hyperbole, it is suggested that this area is now unrecognisable — "I am an alien in my own country. I am in 'Little Africa'" (p. 2). Outside the immediate centre of the capital,

Portobello and Rathmines, historically diverse by Irish standards, continue to attract a varied population. And the new towns circling Dublin, like Tallaght and Blanchardstown, also are increasingly composed of a more multi-cultural population, although applying names like "Little Bosnia" as some have done still appears somewhat over-zealous. Apart from Dublin, the larger cities like Cork and Limerick as well as towns such as Wexford and Ennis are homes to new linguistic and cultural minorities. Although to a visitor from a typical large European city, Ireland's urban areas still look and sound remarkably homogenous, to Irish people, an alternative "other" world is increasingly visible. Actually, as many Irish people found when they worked in other societies, the immigrant world usually runs along parallel to the mainstream culture, visible but also invisible to the indigenous eye.

How have the new minorities found living in Irish society? Inevitably, one thinks of racism and hostility (about which plenty more below) but no doubt, a segment of the white Irish population is welcoming. A more heterogeneous Ireland, for example, could signal for many an end to some of the stuffy parochialism of the past. The Christian or humane sentiment of some may welcome an opportunity for Ireland to offer asylum to those facing persecution elsewhere. For others, the presence of immigrants might be a positive symbol of Ireland's new economic muscularity while others may see it as a sign of awakening national maturity. The problem of course is that approval is difficult to express openly while the voice of hostility is shrill. Thus, the *Sunday World* journalist who interviewed people working in "Little Africa" found it hard to extract many examples of positive experiences beyond the banal, e.g. "I have no problem with Irish people" or "racism exists everywhere" (i.e. not just in Ireland). Even a good news story about the reuniting of a Congolese family in Galway in time for Christmas, having been separated by harassment and torture in the Democratic Republic of Congo, is tinged with accounts of routine racism suffered by the family (*Irish Times*, 6 December 2002).

However, the typical experience of many immigrants is that the local population has not responded positively, if surveys as well as anecdotal accounts are in any way representative. As

Hayter has noted in a UK context, "prejudice against the 'other', the stranger, the foreigner, and especially the recent immigrant, has a long, shameful and largely inexplicable history" (2000; 23). There is a widely held assumption that social homogeneity is in some undefined way superior to social diversity. Dummett (2001) recalls some of the responses to novel "coloured" immigration in the UK and the routine inclusion of the "No Coloured" (often along with "No Irish") addendum to advertisements for accommodation until the 1968 (Second) Race Relations Act as well as the partial successes of the fascistic National Front in the 1970s. Similarly in Ireland, in particular since 1997, there is widespread evidence that the first reaction to immigrants of colour, asylum-seekers and often foreigners in general have been negative, crude and indeed, at times, criminal. An Amnesty International (Ireland) survey found that most black people in Ireland, including black Irish citizens, had experienced some kind of abuse, ranging from name-calling to physical abuse. Those from Asian backgrounds also reported that racism was common. Another study by Casey and O'Connell (2000) similarly found that among new minorities in Ireland, the experience of abuse and discrimination was routine. Government-funded campaigns to combat these acts, such as the Know Racism campaign, also provide indirect evidence of the widespread concerns about the prevalence of hostility towards new minorities in Ireland.

A report about Ireland in the UK Sunday newspaper *The Observer* on 19 August 2001 paints a very grim picture of "racist violence and intimidation" — a refugee from death squads in the Congo reports daily experiences of racism: "I have lived in France and Belgium but I never experienced what I've had here. I've been called nigger and monkey on many occasions." Tourist guides to Ireland and/or Dublin, presumably with no deliberate agenda to distort the truth, warn black visitors of "a particularly lurid, visible and audible racism" prevalent in the capital (*Time Out Guide Dublin*, 2002; 23). Almost ten years previously, tourist guides were warning: "if you are black you may experience a peculiarly naive brand of ignorant racism" (*Ireland: The Rough Guide*, 1993; 27). It looks like racism has changed from being "peculiarly naïve" to "particularly lurid", probably a shrewd summary of the attitudinal change in that decade. Experiences ranging from being patronised, to verbal abuse, to perceived discrimination in the workplace and ultimately physical assault (including arson and stabbing) have been reported in the media by people from African, Asian and East European countries living in Ireland, as well as West Europeans from ethnic minority groups.

Asylum-seekers were a particular target for public hostility. The policy by the state of dispersal of newly arrived asylum seekers in the late 1990s met with local objections and sometimes vociferous campaigns. Fanning (2002) notes that the expressions of hostility of communities were exacerbated by "a more general frustration about the acquisition of local hostels upon which local tourism depended and expectations that asylum-seekers could be cared for in the local community without the provision of infrastructure or specific support" (p. 105). While some locals expressed apparently genuine concern that asylum-seekers would be isolated by being placed in small rural communities, Fanning also notes that expressions of hostility "included an arson attack on the hotel designated for asylum seekers" (p. 105) in one rural village. Demands were also made that new arrivals be screened for AIDS and statements made to the media linked asylum-seekers to the threat of crime. Fanning acknowledges the extremely negative views of many communities and individuals to asylum-seekers, although he suggests that much of this was fostered by the policies (exclusionary) and discourse (catastrophic) of the state and government towards asylum-seekers. This contrasted sharply with the good practice of the NGOs in other cases, e.g. the Refugee Agency and the response to Kosovar refugees.

Of course, racism towards asylum-seekers, ethnic minorities and immigrants was not confined to small rural communities. Fanning relates how small shops and businesses set up by Africans in the north inner city of Dublin were vandalised. In that area in early 2000, "a group of about twenty local men armed with pool cues who had been drinking in a nearby pub attacked one shop. . . . Africans living in the area reported receiving racist taunts from children as young as five years old and challenges from people of all ages to their presence in Ireland" (2002; 25).

Other examples included "a brutal kicking" of a pregnant asylum-seeker from Angola, a stabbing of a Nigerian asylum-seeker
by a gang on O'Connell Street in Dublin and an assault with a
broken bottle on a 17-year old Zairean (Congolese) asylum-
seeker also in central Dublin. A white Englishman, David
Richardson, walking with his black wife along the Pearse Street
side of Trinity College was stabbed and critically injured by a
group of Irish teenagers shouting racist abuse. The couple's son
left his IT job in Ireland a number of weeks later to return to the
UK. Following this case, John Tambwe of the African Refugee
Network listed the abuse he had suffered. Apart from being
called "nigger" countless times, he had been spat upon, had his
apartment spray-painted as well as having his letterbox used as
a urinal by a group of men. (These examples and more can be
found in McVeigh and Lentin, 2002; 4. They also cite the murder
of Zhao Liu Tao in a north Dublin suburb, beaten to death by a
gang of Irish youths, wielding iron bars and shouting racial
abuse in January 2002, p. 1.) A report by the National Consultative Committee on Racism and Interculturalism (NCCRI) issued
in early 2003 noted a huge upsurge in the numbers of racist e-
mails and literature, phone text messages to anti-racist organisations as well as stickers and leaflets in inner-city Dublin (e.g. en-
couraging people to "resist the invasion" of foreigners).

One must of course be cautious in relying on individual
crimes and tragedies in getting a sense of a social phenomenon. Media reports cannot be relied upon to provide a picture
of the broad reality — the media have an interest in selecting
the most sensational events to report, thereby creating a potentially unrepresentative picture. Furthermore, even if the abuse
cases reported are fairly typical of the experiences of many if
not most minorities in Ireland, it does not establish whether
these are being caused by a racist and criminal minority or are
typical of a larger segment of the population. (It might also be
noted that many feel Irish society generally has become more
violent in the last number of years.) It is possible that the majority of the population are either strongly opposed to racism, or
alternatively, that widespread xenophobia may provide a pro-
tective backdrop within which racist acts can occur. Curry
(2000) reports the findings of a small but representative sample

(n = 419) drawn from the electoral register in the central Dublin area. He suggests that high levels of social distance (a dislike of intimacy) towards minorities were typical among the sample as well as strongly held negative stereotypes about asylum-seekers from various countries. To get to the heart of the issue of racism in Ireland and its power and threat requires an assessment of all available and relevant information of course but especially what is needed are representative surveys of the public replicated at different points of time, both to track change (and therefore predict future trajectories) as well as to iron out the artificial and transient components of one-off reviews of public sentiment.

In Summary

A lot of ground has been covered in this chapter, including the Celtic Tiger, religiosity, economic change, attitudes to Europe and racism. Frenetic grasping at topics can often disguise the core purpose of a line of enquiry so a simple restatement of the argument is in order. The central thesis is that Ireland's political system in the past contrasted markedly with most other European countries. In particular, a core political cleavage was that between liberal secularism versus conservative Catholicism. To be on the right in Ireland meant that one's politics was strongly rooted in Catholicism. Modernisation and rapid economic change, especially in recent years, has transformed Ireland so that in many ways it resembles much more closely other modern European countries. The value system naturally has not been left untouched and the decline of the secular–clerical divide means that new political cleavages must now emerge. The argument of the author is that a new right wing is now emerging in Ireland, or rather a new set of positions comprising what it means to be rightist in Ireland is developing. And more and more, these are resembling right-wing values, attitudes and concerns across Europe. Specifically, these values appear to be composed of hostility to the EU, concern about security and crime, and above all hostility to new arrivals in society, whether as immigrants or asylum-seekers, as well as racism towards ethnic minority citizens. A feeling of political alienation as well as resentment towards the political élite or establishment may also figure. The purpose of this short book then is to examine the prevalence of these attitudes in Ireland, ask whether they cluster together as a common political philosophy that has been labelled right-wing populism, and try to observe their evolution over time. A comparative analysis of the rise of this form of populism in other EU countries will be provided.

Before outlining the specific content of the subsequent chapters of this book, one further question needs to be addressed: why does right-wing populism matter? First, it matters, or is at least of interest because public opinion is to many of us inherently interesting; the determinants of widespread political beliefs and their change engrosses many social scientists. Furthermore, most of us have naïve theories about national culture or popular sentiment and what drives it; it is worth trying to systematically assess these views by a careful sifting of evidence rather than impressionistic thinking. Beyond the domain of disinterested enquiry, Ireland's future will be shaped at least partly by contemporary political forces, some of which are only now beginning to reveal their strength. For want of a more original analogy, one may see the parts of the iceberg above water which are visible now but we also need to begin to map the parts of it currently out of sight but which in the future may present many problems. Immigration has for some time been a powerful issue among the concerns of most west European publics; to what extent will Irish politics converge?

At a meeting recently attended by the author, a prominent Irish political scientist mentioned an interview he had recently carried out with two French journalists; they expressed themselves amazed that questions about attitudes in Ireland towards minorities were not being widely asked. At the very least, Ireland's future relationship with the EU will be influenced by right-wing populism. More fundamentally, the pace of integration of new minorities, the degree of acceptance of asylum-seekers and the pluralism of Irish culture will be shaped by the tolerance, indifference or hostility of all sections of the Irish populace. The hand of the populist right is usually strengthened by economic weakness as the old methods and forces become discredited; as noted earlier, Ireland has clearly entered such an economic phase. And finally, one's historical memory cannot relinquish the fact that Europe succumbed to fascism once before; the military destruction of the European far right in Berlin in April 1945 was a shattering blow against that ideology.[3] That defeat continued to present a major but not insurmountable obstacle to the resurrection of fascism. Even if one accepts that modern "right-wing populism" is not the same thing as fascism, its supporters and voters usually display high levels of racism and right-wing populist leaders often play fast and loose with racist language. And as McVeigh and Lentin remind us, "racism is not about petty differences between individuals or nations . . . [its] ultimate logic is genocide, slavery and institutionalised violence" (2002; 5). Paranoia about the resurgence of fascism is in fact healthy and all those forces that flirt or overlap with fascist ideology need to be carefully studied.

In this chapter, an attempt has been made to offer a brief review of contemporary Irish society and its evolution. It has been proposed that some of the changes reviewed suggest that as values generally have changed, so too have the values of the right, so that previously weak or latent forces such as Euro-scepticism and anti-immigrant ideology are strengthening and becoming manifest. In the next chapter, the evidence from a more systematic analysis of Irish social values will be presented. Representative and comprehensive survey data enable a picture to be drawn of public attitudes in a number of domains, all of which are related to a the newly invigorated right-wing populism of several European countries: anti-immigration sentiment, Euro-scepticism, declining belief in social inclusion and equality, concerns about security and crime, racism towards minorities, indifference to the poverty of the marginalised. The degree to which these values overlap among the Irish public is assessed. In Chapter Three, a review of recent trends in other European states is carried out. A comparative analysis assessing the attitudes of publics both in larger, often "traditional immigration"

---

[3] Over half of the Waffen SS divisions left defending Berlin against the Soviet Red Army were composed of non-Germans — bitter anti-communists from France, Scandinavia, the Netherlands and Latvia (see Beevor, 2001; 322–3). Regular Wehrmacht (army) regiments had largely disintegrated by this time.

states as France, as well as smaller traditionally non-immigrant states such as the Netherlands and Denmark is provided.

In Chapter Four, Ireland's relative position on attitudes relevant to right-wing populism is calculated and the prospects of political change towards populism in Ireland are assessed in the light of advances made in other EU countries. The assumption is that a key factor underpinning the rise of these new political forces must be the strength — prevalence, intensity — of relevant public attitudes. (However, other factors also must play a role, including *inter alia*, the openness of the political system to new forces, the relative marginalisation and size of minority communities, the biases and sympathies of the media and the potency of other political forces and parties.) The possibility of the development of right-wing populism in Ireland is calculated and the current political preferences of those most sympathetic to it assessed in order to make tentative predictions about the channels (mainstream or outlying political parties) through which it might be expected to develop. Finally in Chapter Five, the steps likely to undermine the foundations needed for right-wing populism to develop are outlined. Since the cornerstone or main foundation of this political force is assumed to be public opinion, then the question is largely reduced to one about its likely determinants. Good and bad practice from elsewhere will be drawn upon and new research carefully delineating the uneven economic impact of EU membership as well as immigration on different sections of the population is outlined and made relevant to the current Irish situation. It has been claimed that "progressives" have to come to terms with right-wing populism — are there other ways of resisting it beyond co-opting its policies?

Chapter 2

PUBLIC OPINION AND POPULISM

One cannot understand the potential or threat of many political phenomena without a careful assessment of public opinion. As noted in the first chapter, for example, incidents of racist abuse are serious events but media reports of particularly tragic cases will not provide an accurate barometer of underlying public sentiment. The optimal instrument to study public attitudes is the high quality opinion poll survey carried out by experienced researchers, and where possible replicated at different times to enable trends to be tracked and future trajectories mapped. An invaluable example in this regard is provided by the Eurobarometer — a biannual survey of a representative sample of the adult population of each EU member state. This has been ongoing since 1970 and thus provides a unique picture of the evolution of public attitudes on diverse topics across Europe. Another survey programme, the ISSP, although slightly less ambitious, consists of biennial assessments of public opinion in various industrialised countries regarding a number of issues of social importance since 1985. In this chapter, use will also be made of a detailed Irish survey, ISPAS, designed by a number of researchers (including the author) at Trinity College Dublin and University College Dublin and undertaken by the ESRI in early 2002 (for full survey details, see Payne et al., forthcoming).

The Eurobarometer is conducted on behalf of the European Commission and provides, among many other measures, detailed assessments of attitudes towards the EU. The Irish data are presented in Figure 2.1 below. The three graph items presented are CMI (Common Market Index — an index of several questions relating to the general idea of a common European market, used in surveys until 1998/99); attitudes (another composite measure summarising various assessments by the respondent of the value to Ireland of EU membership, used in surveys until 1993/94); and finally a single item, "regret" — assessing whether the respondent would be sorry if the EC/EU were to be scrapped (used to 2002). The percentages in the diagram are those taking a positive view of the EU (i.e. in favour of a common market, assessing the contribution of the EU to Ireland as positive, and selecting "would be sorry if EU were scrapped").

Figure 2.1: Irish Attitudes to the EU since 1973 (percentages taking a positive stance)

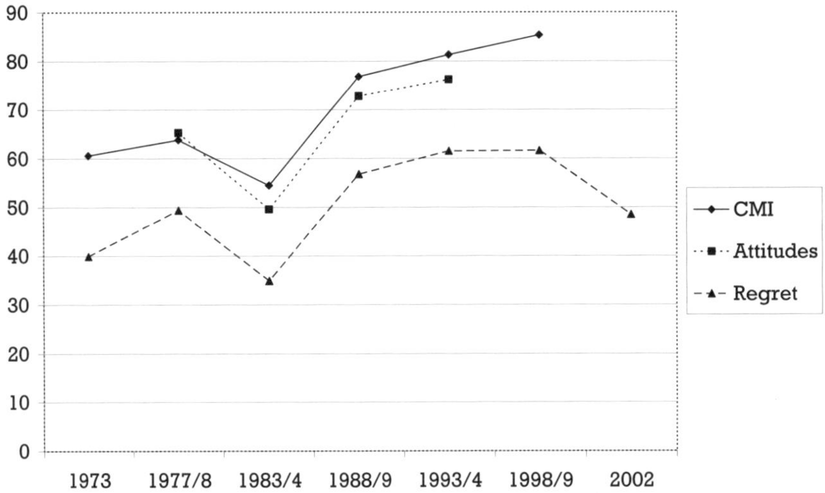

Not surprisingly, there is a consistency across time between the measures charted in Figure 2.1. After some initial doubts in the early years of Ireland's membership of the EU, the proportion with positive attitudes grow but then this falls back in the 1980s as Ireland experienced severe economic problems (the early to mid-1980s were the "basket case" economic years) and attractiveness of the EU model for national sustainability lost ground. With the boom years of the 1990s, virtual consensus backing for Ireland's status in the Union emerges once more, peaking in the late 1990s. What is interesting, though, is how quickly support has fallen in the early years of the new millennium. In a matter of three to four years, only a minority (although admittedly a substantial one) now say they would regret the scrapping of the EU. How can we explain this? For example, the 2002 survey found that 86 per cent of people felt that Ireland had benefited from EU membership. Given that view, why would so much fewer regret the scrapping of the EU? The potential contradiction probably originates in the tense of the questions — virtually everyone agrees Ireland *did* benefit from EU membership. However, less than half would *now* regret the scrapping of the EU. In other words, what we have, we hold.

The perceived threat now for many is the applicant countries seeking membership of the EU in the first half of this decade. In the 2002 survey, excluding "Don't know" answers, 62 per cent of respondents believed that Ireland would be less important within the EU after enlargement while 80 per cent agreed that Ireland would receive less financial help from Brussels once the enlargement had taken place. When asked to rank their current fears about the EU, the most popular were those related to difficulties in combating international crime and having decisions imposed by the big member states on the smaller ones. Ireland has been willing to show temporary affection for the institution of the EU but only on a pay-as-you-go basis. The perception now is that we may have already got the best we could from the institution. While FitzGerald (2002) has suggested that importance of direct payments to, and especially from, the EU may have been overestimated, it is not clear that this message has got through to the public.

Aside from EU-related attitudes, surveys enable a bird's-eye view of other opinions relevant to a potential new authoritarianism. Micheál MacGréil has carefully examined, at different times in the past, Irish levels of prejudice towards various minorities. "Social distance" data were gathered by MacGréil in 1988 (published in 1996); these social distance measures are based on a widely used scale devised by Bogardus (1933) which examines degrees of preferred intimacy with various "out-groups". Social distance can vary from placing oneself at the "intimate" side of the scale (being comfortable with a minority member marrying into one's family) or, on the other hand, seeking social distance — desiring the other person's exclusion from one's society. Low

social distance measures (close to zero) indicate ease with intimacy while high scores indicate a greater desired social distance. In 2002, the social distance scores of a national
representative sample towards eleven groups were replicated
in the ISPAS survey. While one may be dubious of the spurious
mathematical precision of the survey measures at any given
time, this sort of replication within a similar population makes
the exercise more meaningful. In Figure 2.2 below, the distances for 1988 and 2002 are compared.

**Figure 2.2: *Average Social Distance to Various Minority
Groups (lower scores indicate greater intimacy)***

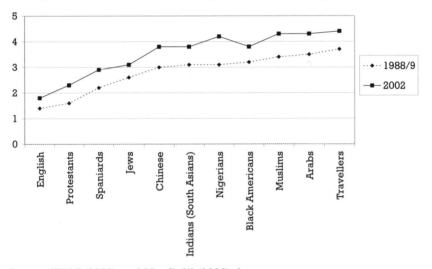

Source: ISPAS (2002) and MacGréil (1996) data.

Despite the apparent weirdness of the task asked of respondents, there is a plausibility in the consistency of social distance
ranks between the two different points of time in Figure 2.2.
Travellers, Arabs and Muslims remain at the furthest end of the
scale and the only change in place across the decade and a half
is the relative worsening position of Nigerians. It should be remembered that Nigerian immigration into Ireland has been
more numerous than from any other African country in that period. And one of the most obvious changes is the general increase in social distance across the board towards all of these
groups, suggesting that one of the main ingredients of right-

wing populism, suspicion or hostility towards ethnic, national and religious minorities, has grown in a consistent manner. If, in the intervening period, "political correctness" has softened the way in which we speak and perhaps think about ethnically sensitive issues, then this suggests that, if anything, the increase in social distance is understated or muffled in Figure 2.2.

What about attitudes to minorities in general rather than to specific national or ethnic groups? The ISPAS survey of 2002 found that most respondents said they found not at all disturbing the presence of people of another race (64 per cent) or another nationality (68 per cent). This should not be surprising since, as McConahay (1986) has pointed out, fascism and Nazism brought overt racism into disrepute. Most people are uncomfortable with accusations of prejudice and wish to be perceived as being at ease with minorities (see Chapter Three for a greater exploration of this issue). However, between a fifth and a quarter believed that there were too many people living in Ireland from another nationality (19.9 per cent), another culture (20.3 per cent) or another race (25.2 per cent). And when asked to place themselves on a scale of 1–10, 1 being "not at all racist" and 10 being "very racist", 32.9 per cent placed themselves between 4 and 10. These questions therefore reveal that while a majority is explicit in its rejection of the label of racist, about a third of respondents tend to take up a position ranging from at least a partial acceptance of being prejudiced to outright acknowledgement of the label. Also, although a large majority rejected the label of "racist" and/or did not feel disturbed by the presence of minorities, there was a high level of agreement with negative statements about minorities. Almost 70 per cent of those who had a view on the topic (i.e. excluding the "Don't knows") agreed that people from different racial and ethnic minority groups abuse the system of social benefits. Approximately 55 per cent of those expressing a view stated that people from these minority groups increase unemployment in Ireland and that they have an unfair advantage in getting local authority housing. Finally, about half of those who offered their views on the topic felt that in schools where there are "too many"[4]

---

[4] Logically and semantically "too many" or "too much" of anything is bad. The question was poorly worded.

children from minority groups, the quality of education suffers. On the other hand, there were majorities agreeing with positive statements about minorities with 86.2 per cent supporting the out-lawing of discrimination in the workplace, 75.4 per cent acceding to the statement that "authorities should make an attempt to im-prove things for minorities" and a majority (50.1 per cent) tending to agree that minorities enrich the cultural life of Ireland. One in-terpretation of these varied responses, aside from simple acqui-escence bias, is that people feel that the rules governing society should be fair but that some minorities are not adhering to the rules.

THE HARDENING POSITION

In what direction are attitudes relating to minorities evolving? It is instructive to compare the responses above with those derived from earlier surveys, carried out in the mid- to late 1990s as Irish society began to experience the changes noted in Chapter One. In 1997, as in the 2002 ISPAS survey, respondents were asked by Eurobarometer to locate themselves on a ten-point racism scale (with 1 being not at all racist and 10 being very racist). The change over time in response to this question is assessed in Fig-ure 2.3 below. This diagram reveals the small but statistically significant increases in the proportion of people over a relatively short period of time identifying themselves as racist.

Figure 2.3: Self-placement of Respondents on a Racism Scale

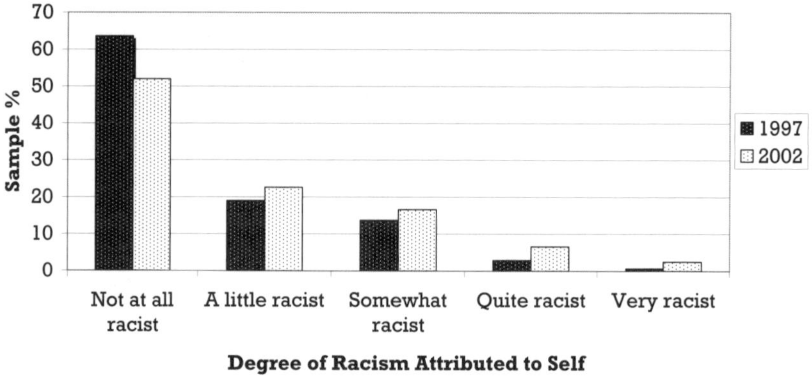

Degree of Racism Attributed to Self

Source: 1997 (Eurobarometer) and 2002 (ISPAS)

In both 1997 and 2002, respondents were asked whether political refugees should be allowed stay in Ireland. The proportion
"strongly agreeing" fell from 22.3 per cent to 14.9 per cent in
2002.[5]

There was also evidence of a growing perception that there
were too many people from "minority" groups now in Ireland.
In Figure 2.4, the increasing proportions of those who felt this
way in comparison to 1997 is demonstrated.

It was noted above that in response to positive statements
relating to minorities, there were majorities, albeit in one case
a slim one, supporting these statements in 2002. In this regard,
there was little change from the responses of 1997. There were,
however, substantial increases recorded in the proportions
agreeing with five negative items.

Figure 2.4: Perceived Presence of Minorities* 1997–2002

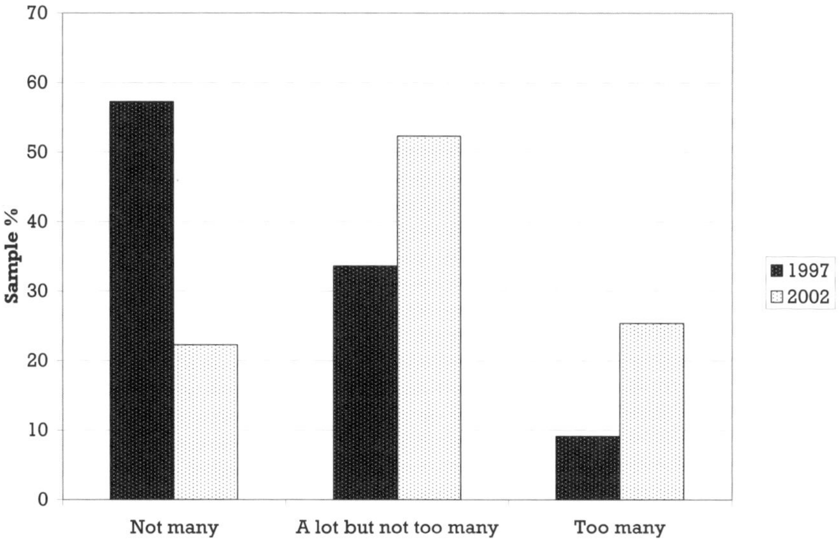

Views of numbers of people from minority groups (*in 1997,
question asked about 'minorities' in general, while in 2002
about minorities of a different race)

Source: Eurobarometer (1997) and ISPAS (2002)

---

[5] It should be noted that under the 1951 Geneva Convention and the related
1967 Protocol, Ireland is *obliged*, as a signatory, to provide asylum for political or other types of refugee where there is evidence of a well-founded fear of
persecution.

Figure 2.5 below contrasts the survey snapshot of 1997 and 2002 on four items, again excluding "Don't knows". For example, respondents were much more likely to believe that minorities abuse the social welfare system (almost 70 per cent) than they were in 1997 (almost 50 per cent). Similarly, they were significantly more likely to feel that minorities have an unfair advantage in obtaining local authority housing in 2002 (55 per cent) compared with 1997 (25 per cent).

Overall, the period which saw an increased presence of minorities in Ireland appears to have coincided with a decline in general sympathy for refugees, a greater social distancing of the population from all minorities as well as a growing adherence to negative stereotypes about minorities and a belief that they are too prevalent in number. Thus the key force behind the rise of right-wing populism, a suspicion of immigrants and asylum-seekers, has strengthened in Ireland and in a very short period of time.

***Figure 2.5: Percentages Agreeing with Four Negative
Statements about Minorities, 1997–2002***

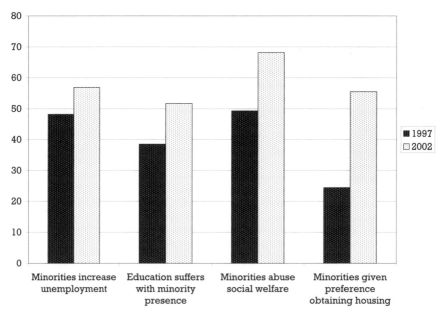

Source: Eurobarometer (1997) and ISPAS (2002)

THE CONTACT HYPOTHESIS

The sharp rise of Euro-scepticism (or dip in Europhilia) in the last number of years may have been partly predictable from Ireland's changing status within the EU. The growth in hostility towards minorities in a short period of time is perhaps more surprising; it is clear that Ireland's economic boom for example required a boost in the number of flexible workers available, including immigrants. Garret FitzGerald, for example, has attributed much of the astounding economic growth rates of Ireland in the 1990s to the "happy coincidence" of large-scale labour demand and large-scale labour availability (in his RTÉ Radio 1 Thomas Davis lecture, Monday 13 January 2003). Furthermore, it is also clear that the post-Soviet world became an increasingly unsettled and unpredictable one with war between and within countries generating a huge amount of human disruption and ultimately refugees. In other words, there was *prima facie* evidence available to the public that the "push" factors generating asylum-seeker applications were intensifying.

Despite the economic and moral grounds on which newcomers (whether economic migrants or asylum-seekers) to the country might have been accepted, a rise in hostility and suspicion is recorded. This is also a surprise, at least superficially, for social psychological theory. The contact hypothesis, first proposed by Allport (1954), suggests that an increasing degree of contact between different social groups, given certain conditions, should lead to a reduction in prejudice between those groups. Pettigrew (1997) for example, in an analysis of a large survey of various European countries, examined the attitudes that people had towards those outside their cultural group. He also looked at their experiences of cross-group friendships (with Europeans from other countries, with first generation North Africans, Turks, black Africans, Asians or with those whose parents were from these backgrounds). He found the greater the number of cross-group friendships reported, the lower the level of prejudice towards other groups. Even those who were not directly in a cross-group friendship but simply *knew* of positive cross-group relationships were lower in prejudice (the extended contact hypothesis).

In Ireland, however, the contact hypothesis does not seem to be working; increased visibility of minorities has generated greater hostility, not acceptance. Why? First, the model is not without its critics. There is an obvious problem with assessing causal direction; it may be that people with lower levels of prejudice are more likely to seek out cross-group friendships. Secondly, as Hewstone and Brown (1986) have pointed out, increased contact may actually stimulate awareness of differences between groups, e.g. Muslim girls wearing long trousers during PE in UK schools. Most importantly, Allport added some important qualifications about the conditions under which contact between different social groups took place: the groups interacting had to be of reasonably equal status, their interaction should involve co-operation rather than rivalry, they should get to know one another as individuals and there must be institutional/establishment support for the interaction. These are serious, perhaps fundamental qualifications. With regard to institutional backing for inter-group interaction, it has been suggested that at best mixed messages have come from Ireland's élites and media (see Chapter Five). For individuals to get to know one another, be of reasonably equal status and co-operate in achieving jointly sought goals, it is likely that they will have to work together, and yet integration in the workplace in Ireland is still relatively rare. The ISPAS survey (2002) found that two-thirds of a representative Irish sample (66 per cent) had no work contacts with people from a minority (ethnic) group, 28 per cent some and only 5 per cent many contacts. Thus, the fundamental conditions that the contact hypothesis requires appear to be absent.

OLD AND NEW CLEAVAGES IN POLITICAL ATTITUDES

It was suggested in the first chapter that traditional religiosity has been in decline in Ireland over the last few decades. The Eurobarometer data allow us to track this change. In Figure 2.6 below, the percentage who said they attended a religious service at least weekly, is presented for various years between 1973 and 1998.

As can be seen in Figure 2.6, the pattern is one of slow decline for the most part but with a sharp acceleration in the 1990s. The causes are varied and no doubt include a general trend towards secularisation, penetration by external media (mainly British), continuing urbanisation and suburbanisation, the dissolution of traditional communities, technological and scientific advance as well as failures and scandals within the Catholic church and its uninspiring leadership, nationally and internationally.

Figure 2.6: Percentages Attending Religious Service at Least Weekly, 1973–1998

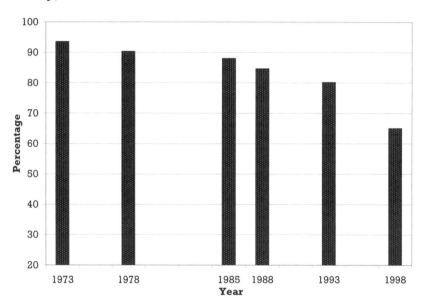

Source: Eurobarometer

It may be protested that Figure 2.6 records a behavioural rather than spiritual phenomenon but in fact attendance at mass is precisely the kind of measure that asserted adherence to one traditional form of Catholicism. Its decline obviously has important and direct repercussions for the future of religion in Ireland but it also has implications for the social and political values of the Irish public. Specifically, the declining power of traditional Catholicism means that one of the core cleavages of Irish society is being gradually dismantled. "Cleavage" refers to a "socio-cultural conflict describing the contrasts or oppositions that are to be found in contemporary societies" (see Kennedy et al., forthcoming). Thus cleavages are the big or structural political divisions over which people do battle in a society.

In many societies, a typical cleavage is the left–right split in politics and this is often to the fore in defining political debate and competing political lines. In Ireland, however, this dichotomy, while never absent has been weaker, and was sometimes refracted into other cleavages. In fact, Kennedy et al. suggest, on the basis of their analysis of the recently gathered ISPAS data that two cleavages, the religious–secular divide and the partition division (i.e. British must ultimately withdraw from Northern Ireland versus the principle of consent by all parties), continue to be the most important ones along which Irish society is divided. However both are in gradual decline, this decline symbolised and also facilitated by, in the former case, battles over divorce and in the latter case, the Good Friday Agreement. They also note that a cleavage they anticipate will "become more salient" is a new centre–periphery one in relation to the public perception of the EU and Brussels. Not surprisingly, up to the recent past, given the benefits of EU membership, the public has been very satisfied to exchange small amounts of sovereignty in return for economic success. However, "as integration deepens and EU policy seeks to extend into areas that influence how each state operates, in particular the raising of money and the decisions as to how that money is spent, increased conflict over the role of the EU may occur" (Kennedy et al., forthcoming; concluding paragraph). Thus, as noted in the first chapter, the traditional positions and meaning of liberal but especially conservative Ireland are dissolving and new ones emerging to replace them. Kennedy et al. have identified attitudes to Europe as the coming battleground — the overlap between this cleavage and attitudes towards immigrants and minorities are examined below; if the continental pattern of populist right-wing politics are valid, then one should anticipate that the overlap will be close.

DRAWING THE PIECES TOGETHER — THE IRISH AUTHORITARIAN

The data provided by the ISPAS survey allow us to examine some of the characteristics typical of those sympathetic to a right-wing authoritarian programme. Social scientists like to think in terms of independent and dependent variables or, to put it another way, measures that we are interested in explaining (that are often mentally modelled as outcomes) and measures that are explanatory (or are mentally modelled as causes or predictors). Turning first to the dependent measures — that is, the attitudes making up right-wing populism itself — is it feasible to think about this as a unitary concept or is there a variety of attitudes from which populists pick and choose? Technically, the latter is possible — one can have a single attitude in favour of a populist position without accepting a whole cluster of them. However, an examination of the ISPAS survey data reveals strong overlaps between people's positions on related but separate items. For example, with regards to the social distance measures (graphed at two points in Figure 2.2), close correspondences are found between social distances towards Travellers and Romanians or between South Asians and Nigerians.[6] Even when we begin to widen the net a little, the high correspondence of items continues; it is found that those who are "disturbed" by the presence of racial, cultural or national

---

[6] Researchers often refer to these correspondences as correlations and positive correlations between variables can vary between 0 (no association) and 1 (a perfect association). The kinds of scores found in the ISPAS survey are modest to strong for survey data — generally between 0.4 and 0.9 — and they suggest that people who would prefer a good deal of distance between themselves and any one particular minority group are also likely to wish for a good deal of distance between themselves and all the other minority groups. On the other hand, those who tend to score low on one measure (not uncomfortable experiencing intimacy with minorities) are likely to be low on other measures. This pattern of predictability also holds true with other sections of the questionnaire. People who believe there are too many people of a different race in Ireland are far more likely to believe that there are also too many other nationalities living in Ireland. And those who say they are disturbed in their daily life by the presence of people of different races in Ireland also have a very much higher probability of agreeing that they find the presence of people of different nationalities in their daily life disturbing.

minorities are far less likely than "undisturbed" respondents to agree that political refugees should be allowed to stay in Ireland (correlation = 0.34). In fact, we can find many associations between different questions related to ethnic minorities, immigrants, refugees and even, say, Irish Travellers. Clearly at a logical level, we may be referring to potentially independent issues — attitudes to groups based on ethnicity, some of whom may be Irish, to people who have moved here to work or study from other countries, to those suffering repression elsewhere and seeking asylum or to an indigenous Irish group.

Some respondents do make distinctions between such groups in their attitudes; other survey respondents, it appears, primarily see linkage despite the diversity of the groups. Almost certainly the linkage is a feeling of disquiet about minorities of any sort being in Ireland and a distrust of the motives of those minorities (for example, greater preferred social distance towards minorities correlates significantly with agreement that ethnic minorities abuse or cheat the social welfare system and 73 per cent of respondents who agree that minorities abuse the welfare system also believe that the children of minorities undermine the quality of the school system). Later in this chapter, the possible causes underlying this view will be explored in greater detail and in the next chapter, how this set of attitudes are found on an EU-wide basis. However, the point for the moment is that these attitudes towards minorities of all different kinds do overlap to a significant degree. In fact, they overlap to the degree that a statistical tool designed specifically to examine for clusters of associated attitudes generated a single factor (or one composite measure) comprising the following attitudes: greater social distance on average to twelve minorities;[7] a feeling that the numbers of those in Ireland from another race or culture or nationality were too great; a feeling that the presence of these groups were disturbing in the respondent's daily life; a belief that those who suffered political repression should not be

---

[7] Social distance towards the English was excluded from the scores as the social distance was low and not predictive of other measures. It may correlate more closely with nationalism than xenophobia, although this was not examined.

allowed to stay in Ireland;[8] a self-labelling as more rather than less racist; agreement with statements that minorities abused social welfare systems, undermined education systems, threatened the Irish way of life, increased unemployment and had an unfair advantage getting housing. These different measures which overlap highly were reduced or "crunched" together into one dependent variable or factor score, best thought of as a crude average of all the items above. This enabled a more straightforward search for the correlates, predictors (possible causes) or independent variables associated with the measure which will be labelled XP (the xenophobic element of right-wing populism).

Earlier in the chapter, it was noted that Irish politics are structured around a number of conflicts or cleavages. In the analysis of the ISPAS survey data, Kennedy et al. identify six cleavages in current public attitudes: religious–secular, the partition cleavage, centre–periphery cleavage (related to Europe), left–right 1 (related to beliefs in economic equality), left–right 2 (related to beliefs in private enterprise) and finally an environmentalist cleavage (pro- and anti- the ecological movement). Again, using the "factor analysis" statistical technique, these six clusters of attitudes can be extracted and given a single score or measure, reflecting a weighted combination of their component parts. Then we can examine the degree to which there is a correspondence between the XP measure and these six cleavages. Analysis shows that the high-scoring XPers (i.e. the respondents who feel there are too many people from diverse ethnic and cultural backgrounds and are uncomfortable in their presence, etc.) show certain allegiances to some of these other cleavages but not all. There is no or little correspondence in the orthodox left–right cleavages and this new right-wing xenophobic-populism; that is, high-scoring XPers are fairly evenly split on their attitudes to the importance of equality in society and also with regard to belief in the efficacy of the private enterprise. There is also only a very modest relationship with old-style nationalism with high XPers being only

---

[8] Although as was observed earlier in the chapter, some respondents may not be aware of Ireland's obligations under the Geneva Convention.

slightly more likely to take an anti-partitionist stance. There are reasonably robust overlaps though with XP scores and the secular–religious dimension, whereby high XPers tend towards greater traditionalism on religious and moral matters. Even more so, they are opposed to further integration into the EU and dubious about Ireland's relationship with Brussels. And along with an embryonic form of Euro-scepticism, those with high XP scores are also eco-sceptic; they do not believe that economic growth should be traded off for environmental protection.

THE POPULIST'S CHARACTERISTICS

It seems we can establish with some confidence a series of overlapping attitude clusters that the right-wing populist is likely to hold (hostile to minorities and immigrants, traditionalist in a moral sense, on the Euro-sceptic wing of politics and hostile to Green policies). What about more general attitudes to the political system? ISPAS survey data included responses relating to political knowledge (e.g. who is the current leader of Fine Gael, etc.), political efficacy (these questions relate to a respondent's perception that they can have an impact on political life, e.g. level of agreement to a statement like "sometimes politics and government seem so complicated that a person like me cannot really understand what is going on"), trust in different social and political institutions such as the civil service or media, and level of political interest. Not surprisingly, political knowledge, trust, efficacy and interest all correlate strongly with one another and, again not surprisingly, we find that high levels of XP correspond with a low interest in politics, not much knowledge about political figures, a feeling that one cannot have any impact on Irish or European politics and an absence of trust in various political institutions.

Examining stated voting preferences "if there was an election tomorrow", those in the highest quartile (or top quarter) of XP scores are more likely to say that they will not vote (7 per cent) than the entire sample (5 per cent). Those in the top quartile (i.e. with stronger XP attitudes) are most likely to vote Fianna Fáil; but of course the Irish electorate as a whole is most likely to vote Fianna Fáil and the difference in Fianna Fáil support between those in the top quartile with the entire sample is small (37 per cent versus 34 per cent). There are small but noticeable differences also between these groups in Sinn Féin support (5.6 per cent versus 4.8 per cent) and the Greens (2.0 per cent versus 4.5 per cent). However overall the political characteristics of the high XPer is not dramatically different from the rest of the population: slightly more favourable to Fianna Fáil and Sinn Féin, more hostile to the Green Party, about the same towards Fine Gael, Labour and the PDs, and less connected to, aware of, and interested in, the political system generally.

The highest XP scores are found among the retired and those with a long-term disability while the lowest XP scores are among students. These have more to do with age and education patterns as we will see below rather than being based on activities of daily life. The self-employed have significantly higher XP scores than employees and among employees, those in the private sector are significantly more hostile to minorities than those employed in the state or public sectors. Also with higher XP scores are those who perceive Travellers[9] to be earning more relative to their own (i.e. the respondent's) income — this will be explored in greater detail towards the end of this chapter but for the moment the measure can be labelled RD for perceived Relative Deprivation. Age, education and income are all significantly associated with XP score; there are more or less linear increases in XP score in line with increasing age and decreasing income and education.

When many different characteristics are associated with a measure of interest, it may be frustrating to try to pick out the "real" or key indictors or correlates. For example, age and education are closely (negatively) correlated; in Ireland, older generations tend on average to have lower levels of education. Which then is the more important factor in its impact on XP scores? This is difficult to tease out, but another statistical technique, multiple regression, can be used to look at the simulta-

---

[9] The ISPAS survey asked respondents to make comparisons of their own income with perceived average incomes of Travellers and Romanians in Ireland.

neous association of a large number of measures with a single
outcome or dependent measure, in this case XP score. This
identifies the following as the most important predictor variables for high XP: anti-environmentalism, low political efficacy,
RD (or relative deprivation in comparison to Travellers' income), Euro-scepticism, traditionalism on religious issues,
older in age, lower levels of education and greater nationalism
on the issue of partition. Income hovers at the edge of statistical
significance also. Measures now that do not appear to be as important (once these above are taken into account) include sex
of respondent, traditional left–right values on equality and private enterprise, political interest, trust and knowledge.

EDUCATION, EDUCATION, EDUCATION

The distinctions earlier introduced between independent and
dependent variable, or antecedent and outcome measures,
have been casually treated to say the least. It seems obvious
that some of the concepts described above as "predictors" for
XP are really and simply associated concepts, in particular the
attitudinal clusters such as Euro- and eco-scepticism; in other
words, it is more likely that they are shaped and inspired by the
same social factors as XP scores, not that they actually deter-
mine those scores in and of themselves. However, as a genuinely causal variable, education is a more likely contender.
Indeed, in a converse way, education has been seen by many
social scientists as the great white hope, if one will excuse the
term, for defeating prejudice. Give people lots of education,
especially liberal arts education, it is thought, and prejudice
can be overcome.

Why should education increase tolerance or lower prejudice
levels? There are a number of different explanations. Some, like
Zellman and Sears (1971), have argued that education raised
people's self-esteem so that they were less threatened by new
ideas and/or people. Others have argued that democratic values were complex in themselves and it took considerable education before they could be appreciated. Lipset (1981)
proposed that education increases social and political participation and exposure to diverse social stimuli. Most specifically,

Quinley and Glock (1979) argue that there are four social consequences of education: it provides people with more knowledge about minorities and the socio-historical causes of differences between minorities; it teaches people to appreciate the dangers of prejudice; it generates increased cognitive skills; and it highlights the importance of norms of equality, civil liberties and democracy. Perhaps. Certainly, the link between education and XP in the ISPAS survey is strong. Figure 2.7 illustrates the declining XP among better-educated respondents.

Figure 2.7: XP Score by Highest Education Level Obtained by Respondents

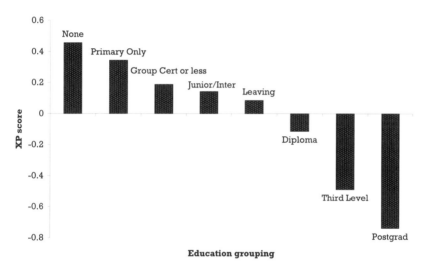

Source: ISPAS survey

The more or less linear negative relationship between education and XP is clearly visible in Figure 2.7. There are some problems in interpreting precisely what this relationship means. Some sociologists like Jackman and Muha (1984) have queried whether education fundamentally changes attitudes and beliefs or just teaches people to answer politically sensitive questions in a more refined and socially desirable way. From a different angle, Curry (2000) has found that people with greater levels of education do show more tolerance but this is not related to the content of what they learn but to acquiring new attitudes from their peers. Perhaps most fundamentally, we might suggest that people with higher levels of education have an altered world-view: through the content of education itself, through gaining the social confidence and knowledge to mix in new, more challenging circles, but primarily because educational qualifications are the necessary, if not always sufficient, tools required to increase social and socio-economic status. Thus in many ways, education acts as a barometer of life opportunities for people; the work of Irish sociologists like Clancy, Hannan and Whelan have made this abundantly clear. It may be protested then that income should be an even more direct measure of life opportunities — it is closely correlated with education in the ISPAS survey for example — education, however, is probably a better measure of people's expectations for their future.

If education is a proxy measure for expectations about one's opportunities in the future, why should it in turn be linked to views about minorities and immigrants? A thorough analysis must examine the real and perceived consequences of newcomers in the economy. In the most general way, immigration is good for an economy, bringing "real and substantial benefits to countries" (UK Prime Minister Tony Blair, quoted in *The Economist*, p. 37, 29 June 2002). In fact, the UK Treasury, assuming that annual net migration into that state will continue at around 180,000, has estimated on this basis that "the economy can grow each year by an additional quarter of a percentage point [worth almost 4 billion euro] until 2006" (*Economist*, p. 37). However, this modest gain via steady immigration to overall GDP needs to be qualified in two ways. First, net migration inevitably expands the population and therefore the number of people who have to share the overall GDP cake. Thus when this is taken into account, the increase in average GDP per capita, "will probably be around an eighth of a percentage point" (*Economist*, p. 38).

More importantly, the benefits in either the UK or Ireland to the population are unlikely to be evenly spread. Research carried out in the US in 1997 by Smith and Edmonston for the National Research Council (NRC) panel can probably be generalised by and large to Ireland. Their research found that immigrants make a modest positive contribution to the GDP per capita while their fiscal impact (paying taxes and obtaining services) in the long term is balanced between costs and benefits. However, within the economy there will be losers and gainers. It must be remembered that immigrants tend to have a different profile of skills than the native population. They will be disproportionally skilled at the upper end among elite immigrants but they are more likely to be particularly disproportionally underskilled. This means that in the competition for jobs they compete especially against low-skilled native workers while providing benefits for the majority of the native workers (against whom they do not compete) by being prepared to provide services generally for lower wages. The estimated increase in the US labour supply by about four per cent in the 1980s through immigration reduced the wages of those native workers in direct competition with the immigrants by perhaps two per cent while adding to the wages of the majority of native workers, and benefiting both competing and non-competing workers as consumers through the additional services they provide.

Thus, increased numbers of adult newcomers will create a modest benefit for the economy as a whole, and a smaller but positive benefit per head of population. However, a small group of the native workforce, people with fewer skills, who find themselves in direct competition with the typically less-skilled newcomers may lose slightly by their presence. While the NRC report stresses that immigration is only one minor factor in influencing the wages of the lower-skilled in the US, one does not have to be a strict economic determinist to see that those with lower skills (i.e. the less-educated) have a material basis underpinning their greater social distance to new immigrants. That is to say, for those with lower levels of education, there is a cold short-term logic in fearing newcomers, whether legal or illegal, whether immigrants or asylum-seekers. (Illegal immigrants have historically found it difficult to organise and defend their working wages and conditions. And, as was seen in the ISPAS survey earlier, asylum-seekers are also seen as having preferential access to other resources in short supply, such as housing.) Aside from the element of economic rivalry with newcomers, there is also the potential that those with lower social skills, who perceive themselves (and often are) in competition with new migrants, may feel a loss of status. The threat to economic conditions is thus one concern; the feeling that one's job, a significant aspect of many people's identity, can easily be done by others, often with poor English language skills, represents a psychological threat. It should be noted that these kinds of threats tend not to be linear or gradual; rather, they are all or nothing. That is to say, it is more common that either one feels completely exposed by one's lower job skills to the psychological and economic threat posed by immigrants generally with a limited set of marketable skills — or one is not at all exposed to the threat but rather finds one's life if anything enhanced by the services provided by new workers. It seems less likely that one might find oneself a little threatened because one's work could be partially done by others. Thus, people with only somewhat dissimilar income and educational backgrounds may find themselves with completely diverse perspectives on new migrants.

This interpretation, it should hardly need adding, is not an attempt to condone prejudice as, say, legitimised by economic conditions. It is an attempt to make sense of or explain the sharp differences that emerge when one examines reactions to immigrants and new arrivals in Ireland. Educational levels seem intertwined with such measures as social distance, distrust of minorities and self-reported levels of prejudice (i.e. with XP score). A model is required that makes sense of these differences in a plausible way. And of course, certain things flow from the model if it is valid, or even partially valid. It suggests that both poverty (involving an absence of marketable skills), as well as social inequality (meaning differential access to the marketable skills provided by education), are implicated in hostility to outsiders. It predicts that increasing absolute deprivation (or poverty) as well as increasing relative deprivation (or inequality) will be associated with higher levels of hostility towards perceived competitors such as those who have immigrated to Ireland.

IN SUMMARY

In this chapter, evidence was provided of a growing Euro-scepticism in Ireland, although from a low starting point. Data were also found which showed that social distances towards minorities were generally consistent across time and were slowly increasing. There was also widespread agreement with negative statements about minorities in Ireland. The proportion agreeing with these statements had grown in a relatively short period time (generally between 1997 and 2002). It should be noted that this apparent hardening of position occurred despite claims of ever greater political correctness and despite the background of an unprecedented economic boom. It also occurred despite (or because) of greater contact with, and presence of, minorities in Ireland.

It is possible that a new political cleavage of Irish politics is emerging, one which looks, in embryonic form, similar to the cleavages in European politics. Existing political dichotomies such as secular–traditional or pro- and anti-partition, although important, may be fading and a set of disagreements centring on an "Irish versus Outsider" cleavage developing. With regard to the xenophobic element of populism, a cluster of attitudes was identified which showed that disquiet about the presence of minorities, preferred social distance and self-reported racism tended to covary. A single factor score, constructed to combine these features, was found to be largely independent of traditional left–right positions but overlapped to a good degree with attitudes to Europe and the environment. Further analysis revealed that the xenophobe-populist felt suspicious and alienated from politics. Thus, they had no clear adherence to any particular political party although were slightly more favourable than the general public to Fianna Fáil and Sinn Féin and was unfavourable to the Green Party.

Among the clearest correlates of the xenophobic-populist position was that of education as well as income. Noting that some of the most thoroughgoing analyses of the consequences of immigration had found a general and small benefit for the population as a whole but a small and negative impact on the least-skilled sections of the indigenous population, a model around education factors was tentatively proposed. Education may have an influence in persuading people of the importance of liberal-democratic values and the dangers of intolerance, as well as giving them greater ease around the new and exotic. However, education and access to it are also important mechanisms for the way in which social status or class are transmitted. People with lower levels of education and therefore generally with less marketable skills are in a greater position of absolute and relative deprivation. They are particularly resistant to the loss of earning power and social status that may entail from direct rivalry with newcomers with whom they disproportionally compete (or perceive themselves as competing) for employment and housing, depending on the circumstances. At this juncture in Irish society, it appears that demographic factors such as education and income may be better indicators of support for a right-wing populist position than political preference or mobilisation. The evolution of right-wing populism is still amorphous in terms of political parties and allegiance; the next chapter examines evidence from elsewhere to provide a basis for predicting how this evolution is likely to proceed in Ireland.

Chapter 3

RIGHT-WING POPULISM IN EUROPE

> We live in a world of spiritually sickening economic and
> social inequality, a world whose progress toward the ac-
> knowledgement of common standards of toleration, individ-
> ual liberty and human development has been depressingly
> slow and unsteady. (Nagel, p. 5, 1991)

In Chapter Two, the characteristics of Irish populists were
sketched. It was noted that the political sympathies of those who
were strongly xenophobic were quite amorphous. Irish right-
wing populism has still not found a political home. This is not surprising since up to recently, emigration, rather than immigration,
has been the predominant concern of most Irish people. Similarly, Euro-scepticism, aside from a despairing period in the
1980s, was not a popular current until recently. Now however,
emerging among the Irish public is a sentiment favourable to
right-wing populism. For anyone interested in tracking public
opinion, this is interesting in its own right. However, for those interested in social and political change, the rise of right-wing
populist sentiment may have important consequences. The political landscape of Ireland will change considerably if it can be
tapped by established or future political forces. Currently, as was
noted, the populist is not clearly politically defined in terms of a
specific party. If anything, Irish XPers, as characterised in Chapter Two, were in fact anti-politics, and quite alienated from the
political system. But what happens if a current or new party sells
an "anti-politics" message as part of its broader populist appeal?
This is precisely what has happened elsewhere, where sections
of publics have warmed to new figures on the political scene de-

crying the rottenness, stagnation and corruption of the system and its ruling élites.

The purpose of this chapter is to summarise the evolution of right-wing populist forces elsewhere, particularly although not exclusively in the EU. By so doing, it is hoped that the likely evolution of Irish politics is made clearer. This is not to say that one should expect a slavish imitation in Ireland of patterns occurring elsewhere. Politics rarely works like that — the future cannot simply be passively projected. Rather, human actors are unpredictable (even if we were to agree that they are pre-determined at some unthinkably complex level) and the social backgrounds in which they operate vary hugely. So mindlessly transposing political events from one society to another is a futile exercise. However, social phenomena do have recognisable dynamics and predictable antecedents and outcomes. The sensible and sensitive observation of broad trends elsewhere, such as, say, the response to immigration in other EU countries, can provide a useful guide to what might be anticipated for Ireland. They will not foretell precisely the evolution of Irish attitudes and values but they may generate a rough idea of the various paths along which change can occur. To this end, a review of the right-wing populist politics and public sentiment in various societies is undertaken, starting with brief summaries of the "traditional immigration" countries such as France and the UK. This is followed by an analysis of the societies that are new to immigration, probably a better guide for Ireland. For resolution, as a by-product of these analyses, will be a general question about the link between pro-populist attitudes among the publics and political representation. With what frequency do public concerns with regard to immigration, for example, translate into the appearance of political forces espousing the same sentiments? Broad social factors that facilitate the growth of right-wing populism as a political force will be identified. Specific issues such as the electoral system and the leadership of right-wing forces will also be considered. The implications for Irish politics will be teased out and developed in the next chapter.

OVERT AND COVERT RACISM

First, the following question needs to be addressed: what is the nature of modern right-wing populism and more broadly of right-wing ideas generally? Rejection of, or hostility to, the foreigner, outsider or minority has historically been part of rightist thinking. As noted in Chapter Two, though (and originally by McConahay, 1986), aggressive and explicit anti-minority expressions are much less acceptable in current times than prior to the Second World War. Nazism, its ideology and actions, revealed the logical end-point of racism and discredited right-wing discourse. Most social psychologists now believe that this has altered the way in which people think and speak about racism. A distinction is made between blatant versus subtle forms of prejudice. Blatant racism has also been called "dominative" racism (Kovel, 1970, referring to "red-necked" bigotry) or old-fashioned racism (McConahay, 1983). Many analysts have noted that this type of racism is no longer prevalent in mainstream discourse. Furthermore, two prominent scholars, Samuel Gaertner and John Dovidio (1986) have suggested that it is not even an acceptable way of thinking. The vast majority of people want to, and believe themselves to be egalitarian and non-racist. Although we joke about it, when people say "I'm not racist but", they are probably sincere as the idea that one is a bigot is unappealing. This represents an important historical shift since the 1920s, when there was a widespread acceptability in racist or antisemitic commentary. For example, a poet as prominent as T.S. Eliot could publish the lines, "The jew squats on the window sill, the owner spawned in some estaminet of Antwerp" (in his poem *Gerontion*).

So can it be inferred that racism has disappeared in the contemporary world? The research suggests not. Rather, racism has changed its nature and has become more "subtle" (Pettigrew and Meertens, 1995), "everyday" (Essed, 1984), "under-the-skin" (Freriks, 1990), "latent" (Bergmann and Erb, 1986), "aversive" (Kovel, 1970), "symbolic" (Sears, 1988) or "modern" (McConahay, 1983). As Pettigrew and Meertens point out, although the theories differ about why exactly this phenomenon has occurred, they share a general consensus that this new form of racism is covert. People hide from others, and indeed themselves, their racial biases and thinking and disguise it in other forms. A neat example given by McConahay (1986) is the objection by many white parents to the bussing of their children. Bussing has been used as one method in redressing the *de facto* racial segregation of US schools. Parents frequently object to such bussing but never on the grounds that they do not wish their children to be in racially mixed classes. Rather they protest about the inconvenience for their children of being hauled long distances around the city, an apparently common-sense criticism. However, McConahay has pointed out that when white children are being bussed long journeys to school for some reason other than racial segregation, no objections are heard. The parents disguise their race-based concerns behind more acceptable complaints. "Disguise", which suggests a deliberate action, may not in fact be an appropriate description since the suggestion is that modern racism is a self-denying one — the parents themselves do not believe they are protesting on the grounds of race.

Pettigrew and Meertens (1995) have argued that old-fashioned racism is composed of a feeling of perceived threat from minorities and opposition to intimacy with those minorities. It is "hot, close and direct" (p. 58). On the other hand, subtle or modern racism is cool and indirect and is composed of a defence of traditional values (and the feeling that minorities may undermine them), the exaggeration of cultural rather than racial differences between the in- and out-group and the denial of positive feelings towards minorities (e.g. it is not acceptable to say that blacks are bad, but it is OK to say that whites are good).

The issue of sincerity is relevant to the discussion. McConahay (1986) argues that whites in the US, for example, generally do not fit into neat categories of racist and anti-racist. Rather, many whites are genuinely ambivalent. They understand that it is important for them to be fair, non-judgemental and egalitarian in their dealings with others. At the same time, they have learned various, mainly negative, stereotypes about minorities, some of which appear to be confirmed by their everyday experience (for example they may see that a disproportionate number of people appearing in the courts or doing badly in school come from minority backgrounds). It is not the case that most whites publicly present ideal attitudes in their discourse while privately holding a rancidly racist ideology (although some do). Rather, most are indeed really ambivalent towards minorities which makes them vulnerable to a form of coded and symbolic prejudice around issues like crime, disorder and "cultural differences".

In a similar way, few Europeans have any interest in becoming or describing themselves as fascists, out-and-out racists or skinhead thugs. Explicit and virulent race-ideology, as has been noted, is well discredited. Far-right or strongly right-wing ideas therefore must take new and acceptable forms. Like its ideological cousin, modern racism, right-wing populism is based on a series of acceptable prejudices — not an attack on immigrants but a defence of a traditional culture under attack; not a racist rejection of dark-skinned people but a belief that cultural differences may be too large (it's OK to talk about cultural differences, not about racial differences); not support for a police state but a concern that the forces of law and order are not overrun; not an indifference to genuine asylum-seekers but a desire to see one's taxes spent well and not defrauded through the indifference of the spineless élites running the state. It would be glib, and wrong, to suggest that old-fashioned fascism differs from right-wing populism only semantically. This neglects the psychological processes employed by the supporters of right-wing populism in justifying their potentially inegalitarian views to themselves (something to which the fascists in the 1930s gave scant attention). As far as they are concerned, they themselves are standing up against a form of fascism, defending their beleaguered and hard-won rights and income against their government, the EU and shrewd outsiders.

Betz's (1994) analysis argues that the characteristics of radical right-wing populism (RRWP) in Europe has several components. It is radical because it attacks the current welfare system (and sometimes the Geneva Convention or the European Convention on Human Rights). It is right-wing because it is opposed to foreigners, outsiders and minorities. It is populist because it seeks to exploit the frustration of the general public against perceived ruling élites. It is distinguishable from fascism by its acceptance of representative democracy and its formal rejection of violence. Betz argues that the policies of RRWP in Europe has had two sides; it has been Thatcherite in its rejection of high-taxation and the bloated welfare state. However, immigration has been the main concern of RRWP since the late 1980s, with foreigners blamed for national decline, criminality and welfare-state fraud.

EUROPEAN CASE STUDIES

France

Let us examine the patterns of RRWP in Europe in greater detail. One of the most dramatic success stories of the (populist) far-right has been in France. Since 1972, the former Poujadist[10] politician and ex-paratrooper (and, it is alleged, ex-torturer in Algeria), Jean-Marie Le Pen has had a noticeable impact on French politics, alternately treated as lout and buffoon but also as sinister threat. His party, the Front National (FN), achieved an apparent high point of four and a half million votes (14 per cent) in 1995. However it seemed to be receding as an electoral force when it split in 1998 and in the 1999 European election, the FN's vote fell below 6 per cent. The successes of the multi-racial French football team in 1998 and 2000 were also seen as solid buffers to anti-immigrationist sentiment. However, in municipal elections in 2001, the far right took control of several areas. It was a cause of even greater surprise when in the first round of the presidential elections in April 2002, far from fading away, Le Pen took 16.8 per cent of the vote and pushed the then Prime Minister into third place and out of the running for the second round. It was argued by some commentators that lack of unity on the left had allowed Le Pen in but it should be remembered that the far right was also split and Bruno Megret of the Mouvement National Républicain picked up a further 2.3 per cent of the vote. In the second round in May against Chirac, Le Pen took 18 per cent (six million) of the votes cast. Among unemployed voters, support in the first round of the presidential election was estimated to be 38 per cent. Support for the far right is unevenly

---

[10] Poujadism was a reactionary conservative movement in France led by Pierre Poujade from 1954. Poujade died in August 2003.

spread geographically, and is particularly strong in the Mediterranean departments, in the impoverished North East "rust belt" but also in the prosperous Alsace region. Three-quarters of these voters reported that street crime and "insecurity" in general were the main motivation in deciding to back the FN. The policies of the FN include the restoration of the death penalty, the introduction of a "national preference" for employment and benefits, the withdrawal of nationality to children of immigrants who break the law and the withdrawal of France from the EU. It might be argued that the French political system has pioneered the manner in which the far-right, though not in government, shapes and inspires the harsh anti-immigration policies of the state, i.e. denying power to the racists by being racist.

Britain

Unlike France, Britain has not provided the distinct far right with electoral success of any substance. The fascistic National Front was, for a time in the 1970s, London's third largest political party in terms of attracting votes. The "second wave" of immigration to the UK in the late 1960s from the Indian subcontinent (as opposed to the "first wave" from the Caribbean in the 1950s) was one of the main issues used by the far right in drawing support at that time. (Enoch Powell's infamous "Rivers of Blood" speech, a catastrophist warning of the threat of immigration, was made in April 1968.) Naturally, many political observers were concerned at electoral breakthroughs by the British National Party, briefly in the 1990s in London's Isle of Dogs, in Burnley in May 2002 and in the Halifax area of west Yorkshire in January 2003. In May 2003, they won eleven council seats, including five in Burnley, and in September 2003 took another in Essex. However, these gains are at the level of council seats and must be viewed in the context of a national total of 10,000 council seats up for grabs; the Green Party, for example, has three times the number of council seats. The areas of electoral success of the British far right tend to be racially sensitive ones (with a troubled history of "race relations") and usually with a pattern of high unemployment in what were once traditional industrial areas. It may also be the case that, as in France, local or municipal elections encourage more extreme patterns of voting than do general elections. The BNP has tried to present a somewhat more acceptable face to the public, including selecting a Cambridge graduate, Nick Griffin, as leader. Its policies are presented as defending "beleaguered whites" ("Rights for Whites") rather than explicitly attacking ethnic minorities. It is also more likely to stress cultural incompatibility as the basis for its desire to exclude non-whites, rather than racial difference. However, as noted, it has of yet made little headway electorally. It has been suggested that part of the reason for this is the first-past-the-post, single-seat electoral system and certainly this makes it difficult for all small parties to push the main parties aside. However, the "absorption" pattern of British politics also seems to play a role whereby the larger parties annex the policy or spirit of the smaller ones and thereby its vote. It has been suggested that Thatcher's concerns about immigration stole the thunder — and the votes — of the National Front in the late 1970s.

More recently, the New Labour party and its ideologues appear to be trying to do the same thing with regard to concerns over asylum-seekers. In early February 2003, Tony Blair told a seminar organised by the Policy Network think-tank that the left could not ignore the "electorate's genuine anxieties over . . . 'insecurity' issues of asylum and crime" (*The Guardian*, 11 February 2003). One of the intellectual architects of New Labour's so-called Third Way, Anthony Giddens, has suggested that the Left can only defeat the far right by developing policies which are "tough on immigration [and] tough on the causes of hostility to immigrants" (*The Guardian*, 3 May 2002; perhaps not the snappiest political slogan of all time). Recently, a "Life in the United Kingdom" advisory group, headed by Sir Bernard Crick, proposed that "those applying for a British passport should provide a certificate showing they are proficient in English, and also have an understanding of society and civic institutions in Britain" (*The Guardian*, 4 September 2003, p. 9). Of course, on the one hand, if the intention is to help newcomers become more integrated in society, then who could object to such proposals, particularly language lessons? On the other hand, one must be suspicious that this is really about putting up yet another barrier with the twin aims of deterring immigrants while at the same time trying to appease potential BNP voters (or in the words of David Blunkett, the Home Secretary, "seeing off the racists").[11]

And after the Third Way, the Fourth Estate has also played its role — British tabloids (although conspicuously not *The Mirror*) have used language about asylum-seekers that some continental populists would hesitate to in public — *The Sun* in January 2003 referred to asylum-seekers as "a sea of humanity polluted with disease and terrorism". Thus although anti-immigrationism has not propelled a small extreme party to prominence in the UK, it may only have been stymied by the fact that its ideas on race and immigration have been (reluctantly?) absorbed into mainstream and even centre-left politics, intellectual thought and expression.

Public Euro-scepticism has become an almost quintessentially British characteristic and remains the major obstacle to the UK's adoption of the euro currency. British Euro-scepticism is curious in its own way; most British journalists, from the left or right, seem to agree that "British identity" is rather nebulous — something vaguely to do with fair play and warm beer. Yet despite the fuzziness of meaning (or perhaps because of it), the defence of "Britishness" from the "Brussels bureaucrats" has worked well for both the BNP and the UK Independence Party.

Germany

Germany, although a *de facto* country of "traditional immigration", especially from Turkey, is *officially* not a country of immigration. The leadership of the Social Democrats has sought to alter the Citizenship Law (1913) which is based on "blood line" and German ancestry to make it easier for immigrants to come to reside and work in Germany, partly to deal with the country's sharply declining birth rate. As in the UK, the far right has failed to make a breakthrough at the national level, partly a consequence of the electoral system (a party must obtain more than 5

---

[11] *The Irish Times*, in its editorial of 4 September 2003, argued that "If we in Ireland are to avoid some of these errors [in seeking to build social integration] the Government could do far worse than examine Mr Blunkett's document . . . and develop a citizenship programme of our own".

per cent nationally for its vote to translate into seats in the dual PR/first-past-the-post system). The Republicans and the DVU (Deutsche Volks-Union) obtained, respectively, 1.8 per cent and 1.2 per cent of the vote in the 1998 elections and in 2002, the NDP and Republicans mustered just 0.1 per cent and 0.2 per cent of the national vote. At regional level, there have been some patchy successes (the DVU obtained 13 per cent in the Saxony-Anhalt local elections in 1998) but by and large the far right has mani-fested itself as a violent neo-Nazi/skinhead movement, largely drawing on disaffected and unemployed youths from west and especially the east of the country. The shadow cast by history on contemporary German politics inevitably means that far-right parties face an immense social-psychological barrier in seeking support. Against this, the alienation of those from former East Germany may de-legitimise the system of consensus.

Luxembourg

Luxembourg although relatively tiny, is also a country of tradi-tional immigration. In fact, aside from its exceptionally high levels of economic success (it had a GDP close to double the EU average in 2002), the other unusual aspect of the country is its multi-nationalism. Over a third of the working population in Luxembourg are foreign, mostly from other EU countries. The far right has no political presence.

Belgium

Belgium, like Luxembourg, has a substantial foreign popula-tion, partly because of the number of large European institu-tions that have made it their home. Belgium also has the legacy of empire, from its nineteenth- and twentieth-century colonies in central Africa, notorious for the exceptional cruelty of their administrations, and now has a substantial Congolese-origin minority. Politically, the far right there has become a serious force, through the VB (Vlaams Blok or Flemish Bloc) led by Frank Vanhecke. Its breakthrough came in 1991 when it took 10 per cent of the Flemish vote. In the European elections of 1994, it campaigned on an anti-corruption slate and took 12.6 per cent of the Flemish vote and two European seats. The stronghold of the VB is the city of Antwerp and it took 40 per cent of that city's seats and over 30 per cent of the vote in the council elections of 2000. Its vigorous demands for greater autonomy and ultimately independence for Flanders (the mainly Flemish-speaking north of Belgium) obviously had less appeal for the French-speaking Walloons of mainly southern Belgium (especially as the VB claims the Walloons are subsidised by the Flemish) but it took 9.8 per cent of the national vote in the general election of 1999 (an increase of 2 per cent from 1995), which translated into 15 seats in the lower house of parliament.

VB is on the right-wing side of right-wing populism and is described by the *Guardian* newspaper's webpage as "fiercely anti-immigrant [and] openly antisemitic". The anti-fascist organisation Searchlight notes that VB demands the forced expulsion of foreigners from Belgium (in the language of the VB, it desires a "humane policy of return . . . to Turkey and Northern Africa" for minorities backed by Belgian funding) and advocates amnesty for Belgian SS men and wartime Nazi collaborators. However the English-language version of the Vlaams Blok webpage claims that the party is misunderstood abroad because relatively few international journalists speak Flemish/ Dutch and rely on biased French-speakers for their information. The VB does not, for example, advocate withdrawal from the EU for an independent Flanders and its position includes support for the further expansion of the EU into central and eastern Europe. On the other hand, concern about crime, a traditional populist issue, is highlighted; the party attacks an allegedly lenient system for failing to crack down on foreigners who it claims make up a disproportionately large number of offenders within Belgium.

Italy

Italy differs from the states above in that the numbers of both minorities and immigrants have been very low. Thus it is not a traditional immigration country. The far/populist right has had two possible political currents in recent years. A neo-fascist party, Alleanza Nazionale (AN), received 16 per cent of the vote in the 1996 general election but this fell to 12 per cent in the

2001 election. The AN is led by Gianfranco Fini and usually describes itself as post-fascist, although it is not clear that all AN supporters have also renounced the label of "fascist". Perhaps more faithful to right-wing populism, the Northern League's (Lega Nord) policies, along with independence for the Northern regions of Italy — an area it calls Padania — include a demand that coastguards should be authorised to shoot human traffickers while the party leader has publicly claimed that the EU is run by paedophiles. Despite its vote falling below the 4 per cent required for parliamentary representation, Umberto Bossi's Northern League was offered and took three places in Berlusconi's cabinet in 2001 while AN's leader Fini was offered one. Berlusconi's own Forza Italia, although rarely described as "*right-wing* populist", has, along with its leader, faced serious allegations of corruption. Violent far-right activity has been linked to Roberto Fiore's fascistic Forza Nuovo (FN); Fiore is a convicted terrorist and his organisation is alleged to have influence among football hooligans and skinhead groups.

Sweden

In Sweden, the neo-fascist Swedish Democrats have turned in very weak performances in the general elections with support at less than 1 per cent. The country is also famed for its general tolerance. Virtually unique in Europe, the Swedish left-of-centre Social Democrats have held onto power for more than sixty of the past seventy years and in September 2002, their vote increased to almost 40 per cent. However, asylum and migration conditions are stringent. While the fascist right has not made inroads in general elections, violence, up to and including murder, has been attributed to a neo-Nazi movement. The potential beginnings of a right-wing populist trend was also noticeable in the 2002 election where the conservative Moderate Assembly (M) Party lost ground to the Liberals (FpL), their rivals on the right. The Liberals gained 13 per cent of the vote (from less than 5 per cent in 1998) on a programme that included a demand that immigrants be obliged to pass a Swedish-language test and should face expulsion from the country following a period of unemployment of more than three months. The party's leader, Lars

Leijonborg, denied that his party was racist or anti-immigrant. In local elections taking place at the same time as the general election, the extreme Swedish Democrats took 34 seats (compared to 8 in 1998) and an offshoot party called the National Democrats took two council seats in the suburbs of Stockholm. Thus, the populist right made progress in the general election and the openly xenophobic right gained local seats, mainly in the south of the country. Hostility to Sweden joining the euro is mainly articulated by the far left. However, the assassination in early September 2003 of Anna Lindh, the Foreign Minister and the "best known face of the pro-euro campaign" (*Irish Times*, 12 September 2003, p. 1), in Stockholm was allegedly carried out by an individual with links to the violent far-right and a criminal record of attacks on immigrants, although at the time of writing, no conviction has been recorded. The surprisingly strong rejection of the euro may boost the populist right.

Finland

Finland, like Sweden and Ireland, benefited from the long technology boom in the world economy. Yet although economically "globalised", it is highly resistant to immigration from outside the EU and also only admits very small numbers of asylum-seekers annually. There is a small skinhead/neo-Nazi scene but racist violence is not currently considered a major problem. The populist right does not have an electoral footing.

Denmark

In Denmark, there is a sizeable section of the public resistant to deep integration into the EU and hostile to the Euro. In 1995, a Euro-sceptic, anti-immigration party called the Danish People's Party (DF) was formed and in the general election of 2001, it took 12 per cent of the national vote and 22 seats in the Folketinget. It calls for Danish withdrawal from the EU and on its website, states: "Denmark is not an immigrant-country and never has been. Thus we will not accept transformation to a multiethnic society." Led by Pia Kjaersgaard, it has found itself underpinning a centre-right minority government led by Anders Fogh Rasmussen and is generally credited with pushing this

government towards populist measures such as reducing benefits for asylum-seekers and forbidding anyone in Denmark from
bringing in spouses from elsewhere under the age of 24 (alleged to be particularly designed to prevent arranged mar-
riages among Muslims). Rasmussen has subsequently received
high approval ratings in the polls; the DF has also claimed
credit for the reduction in numbers of asylum applications; the
party has argued that serious crimes such as rapes have reduced as a consequence, although this claim is vigorously contested by anti-racist groups. A party spokesperson, Rasmus
Hjordt, has alleged that other demands made by Muslim immigrants such as having girls excused from PE and taking pork off
the menu in schools, are changing Denmark for the worse. The
DF has also drafted policies to cut aid to the developing world.
While the People's Party does not have a seat at Rasmussen's
cabinet, it is widely accepted that it has shifted the Danish political agenda and discourse radically to the right.

Austria

In Austria, the right-wing populists have made more substantial
gains. The Freedom Party (FPO) came second in the general
election in 1999 under its *de facto* leader, Jörg Haider, the governor of the southern province of Carinthia. In winning 27 per
cent of the national vote, the Freedom Party had campaigned on
the twin policies of anti-immigration and hostility to the EU. Despite criticisms and some sanctions imposed by the EU, the conservative People's Party formed a coalition government with the
Freedom Party in February 2000 and gave them six cabinet
posts. The FPO, according to Searchlight, has a policy of the
compulsory repatriation of foreigners and the slogan "Austria
for the Austrians" and Haider was quoted as follows in 1995:
"The Waffen SS was a part of the Wehrmacht [German military]
and hence it deserves all the honour and respect of the army in
public life." While in power, the government (including the
Freedom Party) introduced compulsory German lessons for asylum-seekers and quotas for immigrants were reduced as were
the welfare entitlements of asylum-seekers from areas no longer
regarded as zones of conflict (e.g. Kosovo). Until the middle of

2002, Haider and the Freedom Party appeared to be enjoying and building on their success and Haider had even mooted the idea of creating a pan-European, anti-EU platform for the elections in 2004 to capitalise on Le Pen's vote in the French presidential elections. In an interview in May 2002 in the Italian conservative daily, *Corriere della Sera*, Haider accused the European political establishment, the "Europe of bureaucrats" of failing to deal with ordinary people's real concerns such as "criminality, immigration, traditional family values and corruption". The parties in other countries that he intended to link included the Lega Nord and Alleanza Nazionale in Italy (see above) as well as the late Pym Fortuyn's party in the Netherlands (see below). However, these plans and Haider's successes at a national level were reversed following some unorthodox actions. These included a bizarre private meeting between Haider and Saddam Hussein in Baghdad and bitter wrangling between his supporters and the more moderate members of his party over taxation — Haider favoured tax cuts while the moderates wished to suspend them and use more resources to deal with the ravages of flooding in the country. Susanne Riess-Passer, the party's parliamentary leader, resigned and with the junior partner of the governing coalition split, an election was called by the Austrian chancellor, Wolfgang Schüssel. In November 2002, the electorate punished the Freedom Party for their infighting as its vote dropped to just over 10 per cent and the mainstream right, the People's Party, took 42 per cent. (The Freedom Party had enjoyed opinion poll ratings of over 20 per cent for most of its time in power — and opinion polls usually understate support for far-right parties.) Even in its stronghold of Carinthia, the party was pushed into third place. An *Economist* article (in late November 2002) suggested that immigration actually played little part as an issue in the election of that year.

The Netherlands

The Dutch flirtation with right-wing populism showed a steeper rise-and-fall than does the Austrian. For many years, the Netherlands has been a by-word for tolerance. The devastating experience of invasion by Germany in the Second World War shaped a pragmatic liberalism; it is difficult for people outside the Netherlands to comprehend just how shocking the invasion was to the Dutch who had regarded themselves for centuries (and had been) a country wedded to neutrality in much the same way as Switzerland still is. But this liberalism and famous tolerance have been under threat. A difficulty for Betz (1994) in his analysis of the rise of radical populism across Europe was the case of the Netherlands where wrenching economic change and globalisation had seemingly failed to translate into a shift towards rightist politics. Had he published the book eight years later, his assessment would have been different. There were signs of a growing right-wing populism from the mid-1990s. In 1984, the right-populist Centrumdemocraten (CD or Centrum Democrats) split away from the Centrumpartij and in 1994, this party, while doing fairly poorly overall in the municipal elections (3.0 per cent), took 10 per cent of the vote in Rotterdam and over 9 per cent in The Hague. The CD's vote diminished in provincial elections in 1999; however, subsequently a new political force called Leefbar Nederlands (LN or Liveable Netherlands) emerged as a serious political force. In 2001, they chose the ex-academic, ex-leftist writer, newspaper columnist, and dapper TV chat show personality, Pim Fortuyn, as their leader. A year later, he was expelled from LN for his outspoken hostility to Muslim values and culture. Fortuyn set up his own party, the List Pim Fortuyn (LPF) and took 40 per cent of the vote in the port city of Rotterdam in the local elections of 2002.

Campaigning for the general elections of May 2002, Fortuyn was assassinated, apparently by an animal rights activist. A week later, his party, almost certainly benefiting from the public shock at his murder, took 26 seats nationally and became the largest party in Rotterdam and The Hague. Some have seen his policies as a typically Dutch mixture of liberalism and ultra-rightism; Fortuyn rejected comparisons (of himself) with Le Pen as "odious", was openly gay, vociferous in defence of Dutch liberal values and sought to make the LPF a multi-ethnic party (the number two on the party's election list was from an ethnic minority background). His opposition to Islam, he claimed, was based on the "backwardness" of Islamic culture and the failure of Muslim immigrants to accept tolerant Dutch values. This was the ostensible rationale for the LPF demand of zero Muslim immigration, a cut of the annual number of immigrants to 10,000 (from 40,000) and better integration of the two million non-Dutch living in the Netherlands (from a total population of just under 16 million). The party also was in favour of reducing the Dutch financial contribution to the EU, altering the generous long-term sick leave employment laws and freezing spending on health and education.

In the absence of its charismatic leader, the LPF has almost fallen apart; in the elections of January 2003, under the leadership of Mat Herben, it was reduced to eight seats. However, the Fortuyn influence is still being felt — the LPF's collapse was not as great as predicted by some and the main political parties, including a revitalised Labour party, all echo aspects of the right-wing populist message. For example, *The Economist* describes the 2003 election as follows: "Out went the cosiness of the elite . . . out went political correctness. And into all three main parties' view of immigration, openly, came much of what Fortuyn and the voters had said" (23 January 2003, "Sighs of relief"). Furthermore, Fortuyn's claims about "Moroccan boys stealing from the Dutch" were echoed after his death by the comments of Jaap Blokker, the co-owner of the Blokker supermarket chain in the Netherlands, who claimed in August 2002, that immigrants from Morocco, the Antilles and Eastern Europe, were responsible for virtually all the shoplifting in his stores but protected by indulgent politically correct politicians. The country's largest employers' organisation, MKB Nederland echoed this and suggested that the police had to crack down on newcomers to the country.

Greece, Portugal and Spain

Greece, Portugal and Spain have had their own distinctive style of political development as well as a common experience of dictatorship, sharp civil and class conflict and rapid modernisation. In Spain, in recent years, neither fascism nor right-wing populism has had any political purchase and has failed to reach 1 per cent of the vote. Accusations that the police are repressive against Arab, black and Roma minorities are widespread, however. Similarly in Greece, the nationalist-populist Hellenic Front of Makis Voridis failed to achieve any electoral support in the elections of 2000. Sectarian tensions are low and tend to be directed towards Roma as well as Muslims (mainly because of historic Greek–Turkish hostility). Portugal has an electorally successful right-wing populist party. The Popular Party (PP, originally known as CDS, the Centre Democrats) traditionally based themselves on a strongly Euro-sceptic position. However, with the election of a former crusading journalist Paulo Portas in 1998, its anti-EU message has softened somewhat. In the general election of March 2002, its key position was fiercely anti-immigrant; other themes included a halt to the transfer of further powers to the EU, a demand for a crackdown on crime, especially drugs and for the national anthem to be sung in schools. Portas also has attacked the "mire" of centre political parties. The PP won 9 per cent of the vote and 14 seats in 2002 and is part of the governing right-wing coalition.

Norway and Switzerland

Finally, in a review of European countries, what about those outside the EU like Norway and Switzerland? (One might argue that the applicant member states of Europe from Central and Eastern Europe should also be reviewed; however, the purpose of the analysis in this chapter is both to get a sense of the pro-populist sentiment within the EU as well as to try to uncover paths of political evolution Ireland may follow. The countries of Central and Eastern Europe share a common post-communist heritage that makes their trajectories interesting but not necessarily generalisable.)

In Norway, the populist Freedom Party under the leadership of Carl Hagen took 14.7 per cent of the vote and 26 parliamentary seats in the general election of 2002. This figure was slightly lower than in 1997 because of a number of sex scandals and party in-fighting. It campaigned on a platform of reducing immigration to a capped figure of 1,000 a year. Following that election, the party shrewdly supported the centre-right minority government but not as part of a formal coalition and a poll in October 2002 gave it 36.3 per cent support. Aside from its anti-immigration stance, its policy of dipping into a North Sea oil output fund of €90 billion to fund income tax and alcohol-levy reductions has proved popular with the Norwegian electorate.

In Switzerland, the Swiss People's Party (SVP) has had notable electoral success. Gradually, its liberal, agrarian and moderate political roots have decayed and a nationalist, populist, right-wing faction has come to dominate. Running on an anti-immigrant position, the party obtained 22.5 per cent of the vote and 44 seats in a general election in 1999, making it a substantial force in Swiss politics. In the Swiss general election of October 2003, the SVP's anti-foreigner, anti-immigrant and anti-EU stances led to it winning the largest share of the vote at over 27 per cent.

Under the so-called "magic formula", the SVP has historically held one of seven seats on the ruling Federal Council; the SVP's demand for a second seat on the council in light of the 1999 election results was rejected by the three other coalition members. Switzerland receives 267 asylum applications per 10,000 population per annum (compared to Britain's 77 and France's 34) and also has high levels of immigration, mainly from Italy (about a fifth of Swiss residents are foreign). Identifying Swiss fears of being "swamped" by foreigners, the SVP, under its leader Christoph Blocher, launched a referendum proposal to severely tighten the country's asylum laws. That proposal which the United Nations refugee agency said would have made Swiss laws "the most draconian in the industrialised world" (quoted on www.swissinfo.org) was narrowly rejected by 50.1 per cent of the voting population, although accepted by a majority of the cantons. A prominent political analyst, Hans Hirter, argued that "as long as there is in western Europe this problem of asylum-seekers and immigration, groups like the People's Party will continue to push [for tighter laws]" (quote from swissinfo). The SVP improved its position in the polls prior to the referendum especially in the German-speaking North and East of the country. In different ways, both Norway and Switzerland are very internationalist societies, yet their Euro-scepticism probably also reflects a certain isolationist ideology that fits well with right-wing populism.

POPULIST SUCCESS IN A NUTSHELL

The success of the populist recipe is relatively straightforward, despite the diversity of European countries in which it has been tried. The ten rules of thumb are as follows:

1. Adopt a name that sounds (although is not literally) populist such as "People's" or "Popular" Party, or at a push, "National". Alternatively include the word "freedom" in the name (explicitly meaning freedom from tax, and often, *sotto voce*, freedom from blacks).

2. Choose a leader considered to be charismatic and perhaps eccentric — thus a maverick politician from an established party or a media or academic figure. Contrast him/her (usually him) to the "grey" legally trained figures who normally make up the party leaderships.

3. Denounce the corruption and complacency of the so-called establishment parties.

4. Denounce any or further integration of the EU and thus an increase in the control of the Brussels bureaucrats (who can also be attacked under point 3 above).

5. Deny that the membership and/or policies of the party are racist. State that the party is simply defending the traditional culture of the people against an alien influx.

6. While advocating complete religious freedom, denounce the intolerance of Islam.

7. Attack those whose political correctness prevents them from seeing the reality of the crime wave or from dealing with it robustly (i.e. a draconian crackdown). Furthermore, assert that the commission of the most serious offences such as murder and rape, the most routinely worrying such as mugging and burglary as well as the most vague but emotive such as public disorder are overwhelmingly the responsibility of asylum-seekers and/or refugees.

8. Express scepticism about the validity of the claims of persecution made by the vast majority of asylum-seekers (and indifference to the tiny number who may be genuine).

9. Stress the cost to society of paying "exorbitant" benefits to outsiders and extrapolate the ballooning costs of such payments into the future.

10. Above all (and this is where any subtlety of the populist right disappears entirely) demand that immigration, whether legal or illegal, be stopped and illegal immigrants deported without hesitation.

It is informative to assess the countries in which this populist formula has been used with success, say in the five years between 1997 and 2002. (Of course, the formula is an idealised prototype and its use varies in each society. For example, in France the far right tends not to observe point five above. By contrast, the late Pim Fortuyn was arguably the most complete exponent of the fully "modern" as opposed to "old-fashioned" racist approach; hence his heated denial of the accusation of racism, the inclusion of minorities in the party's leadership and the paradox of the party's attitude of "intolerance towards the enemies of tolerance".) In Germany, the UK, Spain, Greece, Finland and Luxembourg, the right-wing populists and far right have made little to no headway in elections. In Portugal and Italy, moderate successes (generally less than 10 per cent) of parties with ambiguous political positions (in the Italian case) have been recorded. However, in France, Denmark, the Netherlands, Austria, Sweden and (Flemish) Belgium, far-right or right-wing populist gains at election time have been spectacular, ranging between 10 per cent and 27 per cent.

Even if one leaves aside the case of France, where Le Pen has been a potent political force since the Algerian War, the cases of Denmark, the Netherlands, Austria, Belgium, Sweden and also, outside the EU, of Norway and Switzerland, must surprise the casual observer. These are hardly the kind of countries one would describe as culturally or economically backward, or as banana republics. Rather they are among the wealthiest societies in the world (they could probably all make it into a top fifteen of the world's per capita richest, depending on how one chose the statistics). They are among the most democratically advanced, are lavishly endowed in the arts and have largely multi-lingual, highly educated, self-confident populations. Aside from occasional Austrian flaps about its border on the east, none are still harbouring any obvious Versailles-Treaty-like wartime resentments. In short, these are vibrant and inclusive societies, not the kind of places where old-age pensioners are left to starve on the streets (as happened during the transition to capitalism in Russia in the early 1990s for example). In fact, these countries, as Hutton (2002) has pointed out, shaped by the "Nordic" and "Rhine" models of capitalism, tend to put great efforts (and expenditure) into caring for their citizens. The "generous German welfare state" (Hutton, 2002: 261) in which "education and health are seen as public goods to be provided by the state" (2002: 264), for example, is typical of the Rhine model, while the Nordic variant is "more overtly collectivist and egalitarian . . . [again with a] generous welfare state [and] high quality provision of public health and education" (ibid). This is in sharp contrast to the US model of capitalism, where under the influence of conservative thinkers like Strauss and Nozick, state expenditure and especially taxation are portrayed as a form of slavery.

In Europe, the use of taxation to lessen inequalities and increase social protection is uncontroversial for most people. But the pattern, curious at least at first glance, is that if one distinguishes between those countries in Western Europe that spend more on average on social protection (pensions, unemployment benefits, health insurance, child support), and those that spend less, one finds that it is among the heavy spenders that electoral populist successes have been registered. In Table 3.1 below, the 15 EU countries, as well as Switzerland and Norway, are ranked according to expenditure on social protection in PPS[12] per capita, 2000.

---

[12] Purchasing Power Standards (PPS): "independent unit of any national currency that removes the distortions due to price level differences. The PPS values are derived by using Purchasing Power Parities (PPP) that are obtained as a weighted average of relative price ratios in respect of a homogeneous basket of goods and services, comparable and representative for each . . . state", (Eurostat, 2003, p. 3).

Table 3.1: Expenditure on Social Protection in PPS per capita, 2000, in 15 EU States plus Switzerland and Norway

Country	Expenditure
Luxembourg	9,235
Norway	8,155
Denmark	7,754
Switzerland	7,575
Austria	7,396
Sweden	7,367
Germany	7,025
Netherlands	7,004
France	6,748
Belgium	6,458
UK	6,048
Italy	5,943
Finland	5,925
Ireland	4,748
Greece	4,032
Spain	3,713
Portugal	3,675

Source: Eurostat-ESSPROS

In Table 3.1, the countries where the far and populist right have had successes are highlighted. The clear association between better social protection and populist success can be seen. So what's going on here? Do good pensions create Nazis? One must be careful of confounding different issues. Partly, the countries that spend more do so because they can; in other words, they tend to be the richer countries. (For example, any attempt to compare Luxembourg's phenomenal per capita wealth with other countries almost requires that the graph be re-scaled). However, that's not the whole reason; social attitudes also play a part and a nation like Sweden whose GDP per capita in 2001 was lower than Ireland's or equal to the UK's, continues to be reasonably content to pay considerably more towards protecting its citizens. Thus, simply by being a member of this society, one is entitled to substantial social goods such as access typically to a quality health service, to educational institutions, state-subsidised crèches and childcare, a pension on which one can not just survive, but live, etc. And of course universal state benefits mean disproportionately more to the poorer members of a society.

Again one might contrast this with the English-speaking model such as the US, and to a degree the UK and Ireland, where the state's role increasingly is only to provide the setting where one as a consumer seeks to obtain these benefits on an individual basis; in other words, they are privileges one hopes to earn, not rights to which one is entitled. Thus, the heavier spenders in Table 3.1 are on average wealthier and offer more to their citizens at a cost of higher taxation (or less freedom from the slavery of state taxation as conservatives might see it). And it is then less surprising that these aspects of the state (being both wealthy and caring) act as pull factors[13] for some asylum-seekers and some immigrants or that high state taxation is one of the gripes that right-wing populist parties focus on as a policy. In Table 3.2 below, the number of asylum applications per 1,000 population for 2001 for each of the 17 states listed in Table 3.1, as well as the US, is presented in rank order. The countries with recent populist success are again highlighted in the table and the overlap between higher levels of asylum-applications and populism are clear.

A relationship can also be seen to exist between the size of the foreign population generally in a country and the number of asylum-seekers proportionate to the population. In the right-hand column of Table 3.2, the estimated size of the foreign population is given; these are necessarily estimates and are

---

[13] The "wealth" component is probably generally less important than the "caring" one. A report by the Institute for Public Policy Research in the UK (*States of Fear*) in May 2003 suggested that security from repression and persecution is a far greater "pull" factor for most asylum-seekers to the UK than is the "push" factor of poverty in their own country. See also Chapters Four and Five for further discussion of the "pull" factor issue.

distorted by the different ways in which the data are collected. (For example, France and the US measure the number of foreigners only through the census, Portugal by residence permits, Ireland and the UK by Labour Force Surveys and others, such as some Scandinavian countries, by rigorous population registers.)

Table 3.2: Number of Asylum Applications Submitted per 1,000 Population in 15 EU states, Norway, Switzerland and USA 1997–2001 and Foreign Population as a Percentage of Total Population in 1998

Country	Asylum Applications per 1,000 Population, 1997-2001	Foreign Population as a % of Total Population, 1998
Switzerland	20.8	19.0
Luxembourg	14.4	35.6
Belgium	13.4	8.7
Holland	12.4	4.2
Austria	11.0	9.1
Norway	10.3	3.7
Ireland	9.9	3.0
Denmark	9.6	4.8
Sweden	8.3	5.6
UK	5.7	3.8
Germany	5.7	8.9
France	2.7	6.3*
Finland	2.0	1.6
Greece	1.7	No data given
Italy	1.2	2.1
Spain	0.9	1.8
USA	0.8	4.7*
Portugal	0.1	1.8

Source: For central column — calculations made by author using population data from Eurostat (population on 1 January 2002) and asylum data from Annex C.2 of the UNHCR Statistical Yearbook 2001, p. 113. Data in the right-hand column are from OECD, 2000; Table A.1.6., p. 306. * Data for France and USA are from 1990 censuses.

The correlation between these two measures — number of asy-lum-seekers and proportion of population made up of foreigners for the 17 countries (i.e. excluding Greece, but including other EU countries, Norway, Switzerland and the US) — is strong (at r=0.67),[14] suggesting that some of the pull factors operating for asylum-seekers also operate for immigrants in general.

THE CONSISTENCY OF ATTITUDES

Are the sort of politics that a society develops consistent with the attitudes of the populace? Ultimately, one has to assume they are. Thus, it is interesting to examine public attitudes on the core populist themes regarding immigration, race and asy-lum. In 1997, a Eurobarometer survey (number 47.1) included a number of questions around these topics in a sweep of repre-sentative samples from all of the fifteen EU member states. In the analysis below, the attitudes of samples from the six states where right-wing populism/far-right politics has made an im-pact in the elections between 1998 and 2003 are contrasted with the nine states where these rightist politics have made either no or only modest gains. Thus, the comparison is being made be-tween Austria, Belgium, Denmark, France, Holland and Sweden on the one hand versus Finland, Germany (in fact the data are based on a sample drawn from the area that was formerly West Germany), Greece, Ireland, Italy, Luxembourg, Portugal, Spain and the UK (to be precise, the data are based on a sample drawn from Great Britain). In Figure 3.1 below, the percentages agreeing with the statement, "In school where there are too many children from minority groups, the quality of education suffers"[15] from each country are presented visually.

---

[14] Strictly speaking, these data should not be correlated as they are not inde-pendent of one another; a small proportion of the foreigner group will be made up of the asylum-seekers.

[15] As noted in Chapter Two, this survey item was poorly worded.

Figure 3.1: Percentages Agreeing that Presence of Minority Children Undermines Quality of Education

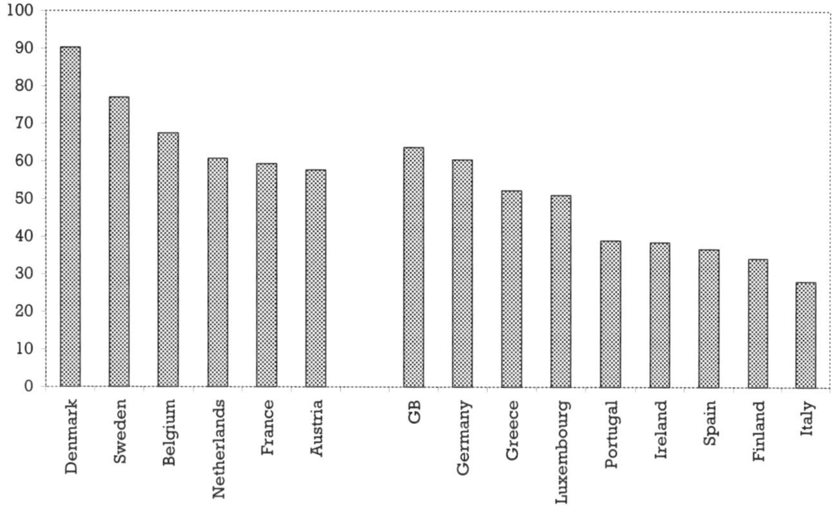

Source: Eurobarometer, 1997 (47.1)

In Figure 3.1, the populist-success countries clearly demonstrate higher percentages of agreement with the statement. The mean for these six countries is 69 per cent versus 45 per cent for the other nine countries. There is a similar attitudinal difference with regard to self-declared racism. The average percentage of those in the populist success countries who declare themselves to be "not at all racist" is 25; for the other nine countries it is 41. Both of these differences (education and self-declared racism) are statistically significant below the 0.05 norm level. In Table 3.3 below, the differences between the populist success countries versus the others are presented with regard to percentages agreeing with nine further statements.

Table 3.3: *A Comparison of the Percentages in Six Populist-Success Countries (Austria, Belgium, Denmark, France, Netherlands, Sweden) versus nine other EU countries Expressing Agreement with Nine Statements Related to Minorities*

Abbreviated Statement	Populist Mean	Non-populist Mean
Minorities more involved in criminality	76%	61%
Minorities threaten religious way of life	45%	30%*
Right of asylum should be easier (% *disagreeing*)	79%	63%
Legal non-EU immigrants should be naturalised more easily (% *disagreeing*)	62%	47%*
Minorities so different that they cannot be fully accepted	43%	33%*
To be fully accepted, minorities must give up religion	79%	52%*
To be fully accepted, minorities must give up culture	32%	21%*
Minorities get preferential treatment from authorities	37%	23%*
Minorities abuse social welfare system	63%	51%

* Difference is statistically significant at below the 0.05 norm level.
Source: Eurobarometer, 1997 (47.1).

The differences in Table 3.3 suggest that subsequent populist political success was at least partially predictable from public attitudes in 1997 (when the Eurobarometer survey was carried out). To capture this in another way, an *ad hoc* measure of "populism" was constructed based on the nine items in Table 3.3 as well as the response to the statement about education and minorities. Specifically, this means that each respondent could score a maximum of ten (agreement with populist positions on all these statements) or a minimum of zero (no agreement with the populist position on any of the statements) or obviously somewhere in between. Populist means for each country's sample from the 1997 survey can thus be constructed. These are presented in Figure 3.2, again distinguishing between the two groups of countries, as in Figure 3.1.

Figure 3.2: "Populist" Score of Samples from EU Countries

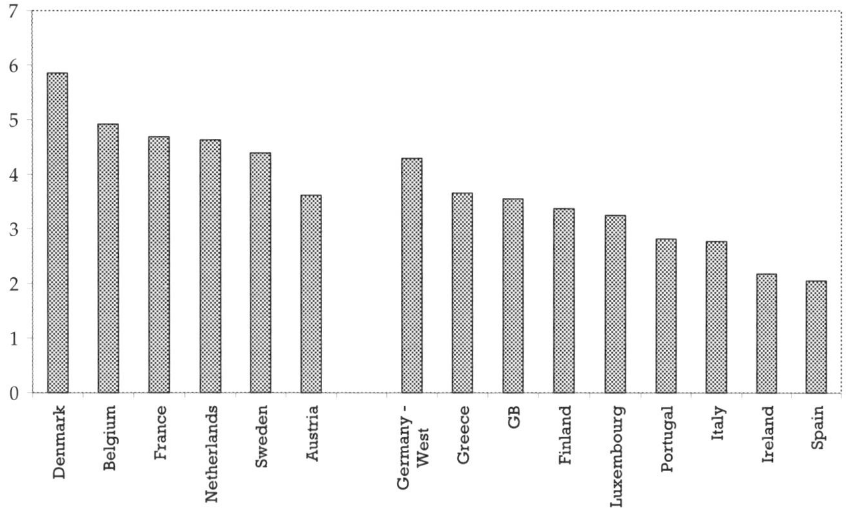

Source:Eurobarometer, 47.1.

In Figure 3.2, it is clear that the relatively crude measure of a populist position from 1997 turns out to be a fairly good discriminator between those countries where right-wing populist parties had subsequent substantial electoral success and those which did not. Within the six countries presented to the left of Figure 3.2, it turns out that this measure also distinguishes the voters of the far/populist right from other voters. For example, the mean overall French populist value was 4.8, while those respondents who said they would vote for the National Front had a mean score of 8.0. The Belgian mean was 4.8 while the Vlaams Blok voters scored an average of 7.2. The Dutch mean is 4.6 while the small number of Centre Democrats had a mean of 8.0. The Danish mean was 5.9 while voters for the People's Party averaged 8.4. The Austrian mean was a lower 3.7 while Freedom Party voters had a higher (although still comparatively low) 4.9 average. The difficulties of deciding whether the Swedish debate over immigration was "populist" and of categorising the Liberal party are deepened by the fact that Liberal party voters had a lower populist mean (4.2) than the overall Swedish mean (4.4) although the far-right voters for New Democracy had a higher average of 6.5.

Educational differences also were significantly associated with populist score in these six countries (as discussed in chapter 2); those who left formal education aged 17 and younger had an average score of 5.1, those leaving between 18 and 21 a mean of 4.8 while those who stayed in education beyond this an average of 4.1. These differences, while significant (in a statistical sense), do not appear substantial; however, "age leaving formal education" is a rather crude proxy for educational attainment and lacks, for example, the precision associated with the educational data outlined in an Irish context in the previous chapter. Nonetheless, the same pattern is visible whereby those whose attitudes are most closely aligned to a right-wing populist position on issues of race and immigration tend to have lower levels of education. Respondents of the Eurobarometer survey in these six countries were also asked whether they believed that their personal situation would improve, stay the same or get worse in the next five years; those who adopted a more pessimistic position had significantly higher "populist" scores (5.3) than those who felt things would stay the same (4.8) and those who felt things would get better (4.3). Higher populist scores were also associated with negative attitudes towards EU membership.

THE LIMITS OF EURO-SCEPTICISM

Euro-scepticism has clearly emerged as an important weapon in the armoury of right-wing populists. The big-hitters of the far right, those in Denmark, France and Austria, have been vociferous in their criticism of the EU, as have those in Portugal and the Lega Nord in Italy. The (Belgian) Vlaams Blok's support for the EU and continuing integration of countries from central Europe is unusual among this political current. However, on closer examination the degree of Euro-scepticism is qualified in many of these countries. Much of the rhetoric and party positions reveal themselves to be concerned about the "élites" in Brussels, allegedly indifferent to the views of the people. Demands are made, such as those by the LPF in Holland, for a reduction in national contribution to the EU coffers (on a per-head basis, the Dutch pay more than any other country to the EU budget — see the *Economist* Survey of the Netherlands, 2 May 2002). The explicit demand that the country must withdraw from the EU holds true for the Front National in France but, for example, has softened in the case of the Portuguese populists. The problem for populists is that the EU symbolises a number of quite diverse things for European populations and is therefore an unstable basis on which to build support. For example, on average smaller countries within the EU have historically been allotted more representatives at a political level than their population size would entitle them to on a crude mathematical basis (it takes 800,000 votes to elect a German MEP but only 80,000 to elect one from Luxembourg). Many positions of importance within the EU are operated on a national turn-taking basis, again allowing smaller countries participation on an equal footing with much larger ones. Structural and cohesion funding to the peripheral and generally smaller EU members has also been appreciated. Furthermore, historically, for countries like Ireland, Luxembourg and Portugal and, to a certain degree, the Netherlands and Belgium, all of which have lived in the shadow of powerful neighbours, the EU provides a cultural and political counterweight to their potential domination. Temporal factors also play a role; longer membership on average tends to lessen fearfulness towards the EU; people become accustomed to its institutions, role and indeed, its not inconsiderable pomposity. Thus, in Figure 3.3 below, in a bar chart depicting national sentiments towards the EU, the more recent members, Austria, Sweden and Finland, are found to be less concerned about the possibility of their quitting the institution.

Figure 3.3: Regret at Prospect of Own Country Leaving the EU (higher scores indicate less regret)

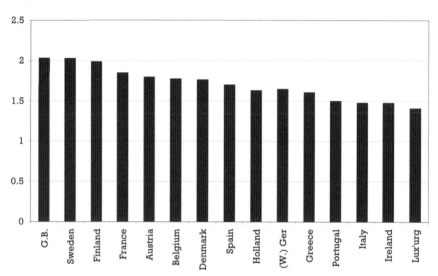

Source: Eurobarometer 57.1 (Spring 2002).

As Figure 3.3 reveals, the association between right-wing populism and popular dislike of the EU is probably quite modest. While on average, the populist countries are ranked among the more Euro-sceptic, two of the top three countries have not demonstrated right-wing populist success. It is likely that Euro-scepticism is contingent on too many factors (historical, geographical, emotional, economic) to be an *automatic* policy for all right-wing populist parties; however, it can and does play an important supportive role in the majority of cases.

IN SUMMARY

What, then, are the central characteristics of right-wing populism in recent and contemporary Western Europe? There is a formula for success around a set of policies, the core of which is hostility to immigration but also includes a measured degree of scepticism on EU integration, antagonism towards what are perceived as the "bogus" claims of most asylum-seekers, a tough-on-crime perspective and a frequent claim that certain types of crime are disproportionately commissioned by outsiders as well as withdrawal and/or reduction of benefits for non-nationals. The "human material" or leadership of these parties are often media-savvy figures regarded as mavericks, based outside the perceived "cosy political establishment". They and their parties have proven electorally successful in small, prosperous, inclusive and generally egalitarian European countries where the state (rather than directly the individual) is heavily involved in the provision of services and benefits. These countries also tend to have electoral systems based fully or partially on proportional representation in which parties with initially smaller bases of support can nonetheless turn this support into parliamentary representation. Within these countries, those who on average have lower levels of education and thus fewer marketable skills (and who are more pessimistic about their future prosperity) are more likely to align themselves with a right-wing populist position.

Chapter 4

THE PROSPECTS FOR POPULISM IN IRELAND

Part of the logic of our tour of political developments in EU states as well as some other European countries in the previous chapter was to gather information enabling some reasonable estimates about the future evolution of populism in Ireland. This was only *part* of the logic — such developments in neighbouring states are obviously of inherent interest, and are not merely bellwethers for Ireland. Even if one restricted oneself to studying phenomena occurring elsewhere only when they were relevant to Ireland, it is clear that trends in other EU states go further than simply providing independent models for possible emulation by Ireland; they also directly influence the kinds of policies adopted in the country. As has been noted (see Lee, 1989), Ireland is a small country and inevitably tends to look elsewhere, often in the past to the UK, for parameters of what is acceptable, indeed fashionable, by way of political ideology. In recent years, other EU countries have also begun to provide models of "best practice" for Irish government decisions in areas as diverse as economic planning to environmental intervention. The very presence of right-wing populist parties in the governments and parliaments of advanced European societies inevitably makes their views more potentially acceptable to sections of the Irish political establishment as well as the public.

The degree to which some Irish social attitudes have evolved in the direction of those in other European countries is the core analytical issue in this chapter. The simple, if crude, estimation sought is the degree of likelihood of at least moderate success for political forces espousing populist right-wing ideology in the medium term (defined fairly arbitrarily as more than one year but less than ten) in Ireland. Political events and patterns, as noted previously, are extremely difficult to predict; the method employed will simply seek to outline the possible forces favouring the growth of right-wing populism and those opposing it. Thus at least, the mechanisms by which the balance sheet is arrived upon will be made clear to the reader.

POST-MODERNISM

In the previous chapter, the differences between European societies and their respective proclivities for populism were outlined. However, one issue not touched upon was that of timing; why is it that populist forces emerged in many European societies in the 1980s and 1990s, rather than, say, the 1960s and 1970s? One factor in this may be generational change; for a younger cohort, the political extremism of the 1930s and the war years was "merely" history rather than living memory. Betz (1994) in his ambitious overview of right-wing populism also proposes that populism's emergence in many societies at a similar time "was a direct response to the transition from industrial welfare capitalism to post-industrial individualized capitalism" (p. 170). In other words, when the post-war consensus model of the state as provider and carer came under attack from forces of globalisation and started to change, orthodox societal connections came under attack. There was "an acceleration in the process of social fragmentation and individualization in the form of an erosion of traditional social bonds, subcultures and milieus, which are increasingly being replaced by a culture based on . . . individual self-promotion" (p. 176). As the old identities and certainties disappeared, so too did the appeal of political parties attached to conservative (with a small "c") social forces such as class and religion (e.g. the Christian Democrat parties). Economically, the transition to post-industrial capitalism created unemployment and, partly as a consequence, a much higher taxation burden. Therefore, radical right-wing parties with their demands for lower taxation and employment for native workers became more attractive to both professionals and the old working class. Globalisation also generated the second aspect of the post-industrialised world; the "coming of a multi-ethnic and multi-cultural world" (Betz, 1994: 172).

In his insightful review of Betz's book, David Patton (1997) has suggested that the analysis therein is similar in many aspects to Hannah Arendt's (1951) classic explanation of the appeal of totalitarianism. Just as Betz focuses on the breakdown of an older order (the post-war welfare state consensus), Arendt in turn had stressed the breakdown of traditional class society in the aftermath of World War I. Patton quotes Arendt: "the masses grew out of the fragments of a highly atomized society whose competitive structure and concomitant loneliness of the individual had been held in check only through membership in a class" (p. 310). For Arendt, alienated Europeans turned to Hitler and nationalist-totalitarianism to overcome their powerful longing for group membership. For Betz, on the other hand, alienated Europeans turn to radical right-wing parties to fully free themselves from the old collectivist trappings like class and religion.

There are a number of problems with Betz's analysis. It fails to tell us why the Tories in the UK, for example, who provide a virtual caricature of a political force determined to strip away the welfare state and usher in a "post-industrial individualised" society did not also play the race/immigration card to the same degree as continental right-wing populists, although some certainly did. There is also an unsatisfactory circular logic to the argument whereby the forces of globalisation and individualisation are alleged to have ushered in, as a reaction, a widespread public desire for greater globalisation and individualisation. And finally one worries about explanations that are faintly nostalgic; that once we had certainty and now we have chaos. As Pearson (1983) has convincingly shown with regard to the public perception of a more secure crime-free society somewhere vaguely in the past, it rarely feels to those living through a particular era that their existences are fixed by stable bonds. It is commonplace for every generation to feel that they are living through some qualitatively new period where all previous social rules are forgotten (e.g. Dickens's "it was the best of times, it was the worst of times, it was the age of wisdom, it was the age of foolishness"). One might just as easily suggest that those living in the 1960s (sexual revolution) or the 1970s (the oil crisis) should have had a sense of atomisation and hyper-individualism.

However, if one credits rapid social change towards post-modernism and globalisation as at least facilitating the circumstances in which right-wing populism can grow, then the whirlwind transformation of Irish society in the 1990s (see Chapter One) and the very rapid decline of Catholic Church power must be regarded as creating relatively very fertile political ground. Aside from post-modernism, what then of Euro-scepticism in the medium term?

THE LIMITS OF IRISH EURO-SCEPTICISM

In Ireland's case, Euro-scepticism is unlikely to be a big vote-winner. In Chapter Three, it was noted that Euro-scepticism has had a varying appeal in other European societies, ranging from the measured to the dominant. Although we saw in Chapter Two that Euro-scepticism is growing relatively quickly in Ireland, it is clear that the baseline level of pro-EU support is still too high for it to play an important role in the medium term as a populist policy. This will undoubtedly change as the power of the EU is extended further and formalised (e.g. with the possibility of a new constitution) and as the patterns of benefits and payments alter with the accession of some or all of the current applicant states. However, the memory of positive factors associated with membership will provide a bulwark resistant to short-term erosion. It would not be entirely unfair to condense the debate in the Nice Treaty Referenda I and II to the Yes side stressing the positive memory of the EU in the past while the No side played to the fears of an unknown future EU. Euro-scepticism's development in Ireland will be a function of the net outcome of public sentiment about the positive past and negative future.

THE ECONOMY AND CHANGE IN IRELAND

A third factor regularly offered as a cause of right-wing populism is the general state of the economy and economic growth.
The pessimism surrounding the prospects for the world economy has already been alluded to in Chapter One. The issue
thus for Ireland in the medium term is its economic prospects
and how these might influence (catapult forward or retard)
various political forces. Economic change in Ireland was explosive throughout the 1990s, especially in the latter half. Figure
4.1 reminds the reader of the changes in the Irish GNP rate in
that period.

*Figure 4.1: GNP per annum increase (recorded and
estimated) for Ireland, 1998–2003, at constant (1995) prices*

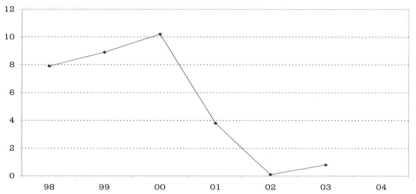

Source: Monthly Economic Bulletin, issued by Minister for Finance, August
2003. GNP figure for 2003 is a CSO estimate for the first quarter of the year.

It is apparent from Figure 4.1 that growth rates have fluctuated
wildly. On the positive side, the rates of growth were remark-
able in the good years. Even on its way down in 2001, it must
have still looked remarkably healthy to other EU countries.
However, the decline in the rate of growth has been faster in
Ireland than any other country. While the cause for this is positive (only a growth rate so high can normally fall so steeply),
there is the issue of relative change; many people may have
become accustomed to big annual increases in income (or at
least nominal changes since inflation of course ate into much of
what was gained). Further public disappointment may accom-

pany the equally serious shortfall in government revenue; the years of record surpluses meant government largesse could ease the pain. However, in July of 2003, the government was warning of further spending cutbacks and a tough end-of-year budget as tax revenues fell again. The "Stability and Growth" pact within the euro-zone commits governments to keep their spending deficit within 3 per cent of GDP; that this issue is even being discussed now in an Irish context so soon after the boom is a sign of the speed of the setback.

What kind of disgruntlement is engendered by a return to "only" solid and steady progress after the high-flying years? Is it likely to produce an equivalent kind of disappointment as the decline from normal growth to sharp economic contraction (in absolute terms) has done elsewhere? And is this the kind of disappointment that translates into support for the far right? Inevitably, the case of Weimar Germany comes to mind when thinking about such questions. In particular, one recalls the infamous hyper-inflation, the previously unknown levels of unemployment and the lost lifetime savings that preceded the rise of Nazism. But of course, such an economic catastrophe was unique for all intents and purposes in the advanced liberal democracies. The environment was also exceptional; the US underwent severe depression and economic trauma in the 1930s; and yet the result was the leftish New Deal Roosevelt government. By contrast, the bitterly resented Treaty of Versailles was part of the social-psychological context for German fascism. But most importantly, as we saw in Chapter Three, the populist successes of the late 1990s and early in the new century have not replicated the dominating example of inter-war Germany. In fact, precisely the opposite; the successes have been registered among more economically stable and successful European societies. Figure 4.2 presents a bar-chart of the PPPs (purchasing power parities; these income measurements strip out differences in the cost-of-living as well as fluctuations in the exchange rates to enable sensible comparison) of fifteen EU countries plus Norway and Switzerland.

Figure 4.2: PPPs ("current") for 2002 in 17 European Countries

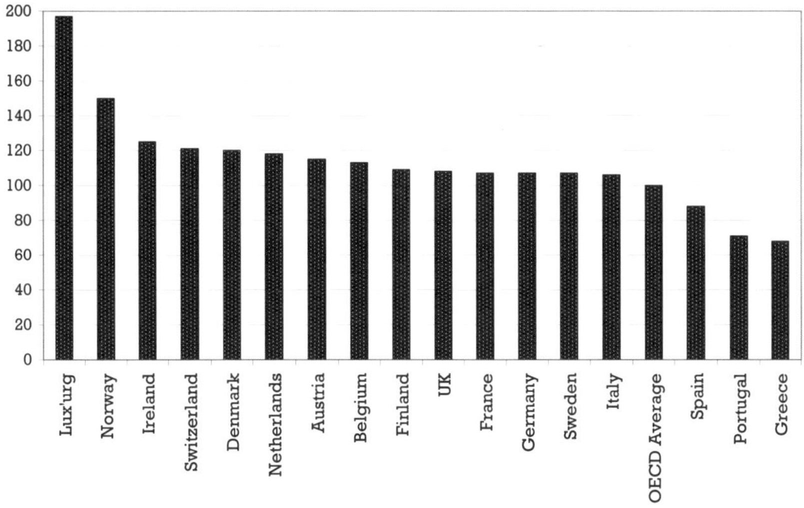

Source: OECD, 2003.

Countries in which right-wing populism has been relatively successful in recent years are to be found among the OECD's
wealthiest. In Figure 4.2, Norway, Switzerland, Denmark, the
Netherlands, Austria and Belgium are among the seven top-
scoring PPP levels for 2002 (and Luxembourg can be considered unique while Ireland's economic success has been very
recent). Furthermore, these high standards of living have been
constant, rather than intermittent features in the lives of those
living in these societies. The unemployment rate in five of the
six countries mentioned above was less than 5 per cent in 2000
(the exception was Belgium with a rate of 11.0 per cent; OECD,
2001) and the GDP growth rates averaged across the 1990s at
respectable rates of 3.2 per cent (Norway), 2.8 per cent (Netherlands), 2.3 per cent (Denmark), 2.1 per cent (Austria and Belgium) and 1.1 per cent (Switzerland) (OECD, 2003). So there is
no evidence that the modern pattern of populism is a response
to a troubled national economy. It seems more likely, given the
evidence in Chapters Two and Three, that it is the response of
sections of the less well-off among populations accustomed to
high levels of state social provision, to a perceived threat to
their standard-of-living from newcomers in society. In Ireland,

therefore, it is not all that clear that even relatively substantial changes in levels of economic growth should change the prospects for populism. For example, higher levels of wealth might encourage greater feelings of social confidence but could also act as pull factors for immigrants and asylum-seekers. (That asylum-seekers should be attracted, all things being equal, by societies with higher standards of living should not surprise. If one had to flee a despotic regime in Ireland tomorrow, would one's destination be more likely to be Canada or Mexico? However, see also the footnote on page 72 regarding UK evidence around pull factors; asylum-seekers there have generally been more concerned about fleeing repression than seeking wealth.)

IMMIGRATION AND ASYLUM-SEEKERS

And this leads us neatly to what is and has been *the* important issue in the rise of populism and the open secret of its success in various European countries — the fear of immigrants and asylum-seekers arriving in substantial numbers. In Table 3.2 in the previous chapter, the connection between asylum-seeker numbers and the success of populism was illustrated by highlighting those countries, in bold, where the populists had experienced political success. Those societies, it was noted, had in the period 1997–2001 received more asylum-seeker applications on average per 1,000 population than the societies where populism was weaker. One of the points not dwelt upon was that, along with the exceptional state of Luxembourg, Ireland was unusual in that it found itself among those societies more sought out by asylum-seekers yet had not experienced the rise of populism. Indeed, in public attitudes (see Figure 3.2 in previous chapter), it was firmly placed among the non-populists. But timing once again is an important consideration. In Chapter One, the "phenomenal" change in numbers of asylum-seekers in Ireland was noted. The timing of the change is captured in Figure 4.3 below.

Figure 4.3: Number of new asylum applications submitted in Ireland, 1994–2002

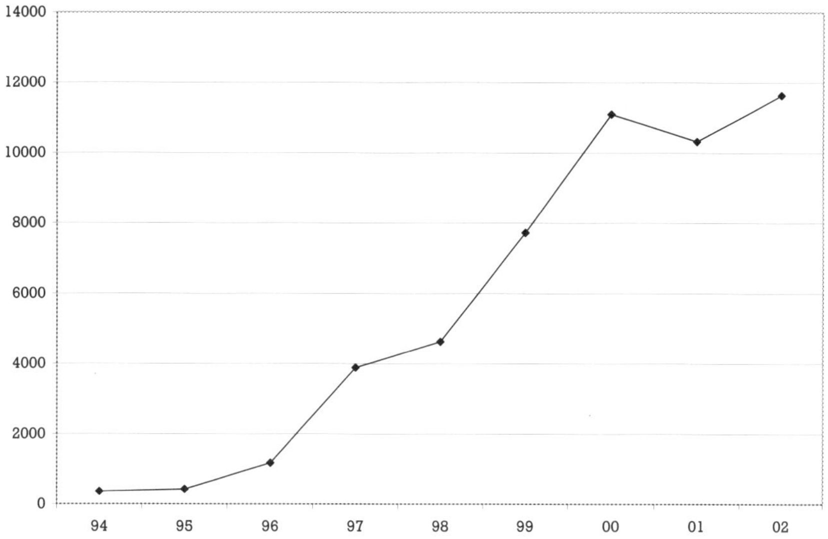

Source: UNHCR Statistical Yearbook 2001, Annex C.2. Figure for 2002 from the UNHCR website (statistics section).

There are reasonable grounds for thinking on the basis of the data in Figure 4.3 that asylum-seekers only became a noticeable or an identifiable reality, often via the media, for most Irish citizens from 1997 or 1998 onwards. Therefore one must assess the change occurring in Irish attitudes since then and the *meaning* one should attribute to the change. In Chapter Two, for example, Irish survey data were made more meaningful by comparing them where possible to the results of similar questions asked at a different (earlier) time in Ireland. However, another way to make survey data meaningful is to make comparisons of views in Ireland with those elsewhere. In particular, the ISPAS survey of early 2002 replicated several questions relating to minorities previously asked in 1997. In 1997, 38 per cent of Irish people had agreed that "In school where there are too many children from minority groups, the quality of education suffers". In Chapter Three, it was noted that the mean percentage agreement for populist[16] countries in 1997 in response to this item was 69 per cent while it was 45 per cent for non-populist countries. The Irish sample of 2002 had moved up to 52 per cent, well above the non-populist mean and into a transition place between populism and non-populism. Furthermore, in 1997, 44 per cent of Irish respondents had scored themselves as a "1" on a self-placement racism scale from 1 to 10, indicating the lowest level of racism. This compared with 41 per cent of non-populist countries and 25 per cent for populist countries. By 2002, in the ISPAS survey, the Irish sample of respondents placing themselves at the point of least racism on a scale had fallen to 32 per cent, closer to the populist mean of a few years previously than the non-populist. Those agreeing, among the Irish samples, that "minorities get preferential treatment from the authorities"[17] increased from 25 per cent to 56 per cent from 1997 to 2002 compared to a non-populist mean of 23 per cent in 1997 and a populist mean of 37 per cent in the same year. And finally, while 49 per cent of Irish respondents in 1997 agreed that "minorities abuse the social welfare system" compared to 51 per cent of non-populists and 63 per cent of populists, the proportion of Irish respondents agreeing with the same statement in 2002 was 68 per cent, well above the populist mean of four years previously. In other words, it is clear that in five years, and with the experience of increased numbers of asylum-seekers and immigrants, Irish attitudes on some key items towards minorities have moved, in a negative fashion, either towards or indeed well beyond the levels characterising populist countries a few years previously.

FOCUS GROUP EVIDENCE

The figures above are based on the analysis of fixed or structured surveys. However, as is commonly noted, these types of structured surveys, in which the range of responses is tightly

---

[16] Austria, Belgium, Denmark, France, Netherlands and (with some hesitation) Sweden.

[17] However, the wording here was changed so that the 2002 item referred to "preferential treatment in housing". The 1997 item had not been specific about the manner in which the authorities had been preferential.

prescribed, have a tendency to exchange rigour for richness. The "coldness" of a survey also makes it difficult for rapport to be achieved with the respondent. Alternative methodologies such as unstructured interviews and focus groups can be used to flesh out the views behind the statistics of a survey analysis. As a precursor to running the ISPAS survey (on which the 2002 survey figures above are based), the questions relating to minorities were discussed in three focus group meetings in Dublin in early July 2001, where the experience of multiculturalism among participants was relatively common.[18] These were: (1) a working-class area of West Dublin; (2) an inner-city economically deprived area of North Dublin (Dublin 1 postcode); and (3) a middle class/professional group employed by a multi-national US company in the greater Dublin area. These are loosely representative of the areas of Dublin, mentioned in Chapter One, where newcomers have changed the traditional homogeneity of the population. The group sizes ranged from six to eight and were gender-mixed except in the first instance, which was exclusively female. While accepting that the social representativeness of the groups must remain uncertain, the class differences in perspective that emerged were very strong. The middle-class group offered very positive views of working with people of different nationalities and ethnicities and expressed regret that work and social mixing was not greater (although their interaction was based on the working rather than residential environment). For example, one respondent commented, without contradiction from other members of the focus group:

> It probably sounds a bit wonderlandish when we say we haven't seen any racism. I actually haven't. I actually haven't . . . We're very lucky with the working environment and the people who are in it . . . It is sort of, everybody gets on with each other.

They regarded those who were hostile to immigrants and asylum-seekers as "hypocrites".

---

[18] The focus groups were organised and facilitated by an experienced social researcher, Ms Caroline Corr.

The contrast was very sharp with the groups from more economically deprived backgrounds. A small part of the hostility was clearly based on what one might call "old-fashioned racism" and the feeling of threat of intimacy with outsiders. For example, participants alluded to the risk of infection from disease they perceived from those "coming off the boats and planes" and suggested quarantine or immunisation. In part aligned to this was the sexual threat some women (in the all-women group) felt towards all non-white or non-Irish men (examples cited included Italians, Spaniards, Blacks, Algerians). However the main source of their negative feelings and most of the conversation was on the perceived ease of access and abundance of state benefits for asylum-seekers, especially in the area of housing. The following quotations provide illustrations of the strong feelings recorded in the focus groups in less well-off areas. (The frequent equation of "blacks" with "refugees" was made by the focus group members, not the facilitator.)

> I think people wouldn't have a problem with the refugees if they went up the ladder like the rest of us. Started like the rest of us in Ballymun. . . . But they're just coming and they're jumping the line and they're getting the houses with the result people are getting very prejudiced against them. . . . Everybody else is fighting hard with the council and yet they can come into the country and they're given places to live. (Respondent 5 from focus group 1 (R5, FG1))

> It's costing the government . . . 52 million a year to keep refugees in the country. It's madness when our own . . . is homeless. . . . If they want to move into our country and live the way we live they should start the way we do. Go up and stand in queues, stand in the Corporation, start off in a scrappy little flat, not just walk in and get these lovely houses. (R6, FG1)

> There's a lot more Dublin people on the streets than there are coloured people, which I thought was very, very bad . . . My daughter tried to get into _____ school . . . but three coloured people could walk in ahead of her into that school. And they had just come into the country, they hadn't been in the country a month . . . I think it's the unfairness of it that's

making us prejudiced. We wouldn't be prejudiced otherwise. But it's the unfairness of it. (R2, FG1)

I know a refugee from Russia and they have their own place and they pay someone to come in and clean it. Now how poor is that? (R4, FG1)

Well I think it's sickening a black person getting a house before an Irish person. I'm on that list a year and a half and I'm told no. They can get their own house, walk in and get it. It's sickening. (R7, FG1)

The money they get for their houses as well, they don't have to pay as much as we do. I don't mind working at my job but I don't see why they shouldn't pay as much as me. . . . There was this fella and him and his girlfriend were looking for a flat. And they kept on saying to him no we don't have anything for you. I mean if he was black they'd have a house for him but if he was white, they wouldn't have a place for him . . . I don't think it's right. (R1, FG2)

A year and a half in the country and they have a house in Crumlin. I've been in Ireland all my life and I'd have to wait years for a house in Crumlin. That's what annoys me, I'm not racist as such but I get annoyed when I see them getting more than we're getting and getting first preference. (R3, FG2)

The transformation of the Butlin's holiday camp at Mosney outside Dublin into an accommodation centre for asylum-seekers was cited as a particularly emotional issue.

Like where's Mosney gone? I classed that as my childhood home. That's where I was brought every year of my life when I was a kid. You can't go there now. (R6, FG1)

And then Mosney? Now that wasn't fair. A lot of people can't afford to go away on holidays and we used to go there every year and I used to bring the baby down there for her birthday and now it's gone. (R5, FG2)

You know Butlins? Well that's gone now. All the refugees are living there now in those lovely apartments. (R1, FG2)

Although housing was the main source of grievance, there were other concerns about the alleged abuse of the welfare system.

Social — they only have come into the country and they want
to know what day is the social. Every one of them knows what
day is the social. . . . They are getting their breakfast, dinner,
tea, they have their central heating, their hot water, their TVs,
they have their videos. They are getting £15 per person off
the welfare as well. "More money in Ireland. More money in
Ireland." They'll tell you that. (R5, FG1)

They are getting handouts from everywhere. (R6, FG1)

There is scams going on. I don't think anyone can deny that.
(R8, FG1)

The stressing of cultural difference characteristic of modern racism was expressed around the issue of manners versus igno-
rance.

They're ignorant. It's not that they expect, they demand. . . .
I treat people the way I like to be treated but an awful lot of
refugees, you just couldn't be nice to them. You were like
dirt underneath their feet. And why do they have big scars
all over their face? (R5, FG1)

They lived the other side of me and honest to God, the noise
and the carry on and the screaming and the shouting, it was
unbelievable . . . even the neighbours and all, and they
would start fighting among themselves. (R9, FG1)

I work with a Latvian . . . They can barely speak English.
And [in Parnell Street] do you see the way the refugees
carry their children? I'd be scared sometimes that the children will get whiplash. (R1, FG1)

No matter what time of the day or night on O'Connell Street,
they are in bunches and I mean literally bunches across . . . I
don't know what kind of lingo they used but I wasn't being
called a lady . . . I find them the most ignorant lot of people
that I have ever come across. (R4, FG1)

Sometimes you can't walk down the street without all of them
being there . . . The women are very ignorant. (R1, FG2)

I think a lot of them could have a problem with the language
and that and they might come across as ignorant but they
just don't know. I worked for Vietnamese and they were
dead ignorant, treated me like dirt. (R3, FG2)

> They don't even understand our money . . . they can't drive
> either. (R5, FG2)

But also characteristic of modern racism is its denial, sometimes
strenuous, sometimes ambiguous. Most said they were not racist.

> Their skin wouldn't make any difference. . . . I've nothing
> against them, I'm not prejudiced in any shape or form. (R2,
> FG1)

> I wouldn't be prejudiced in any way against any coloured
> person. . . . I don't mind what way people live around here
> as long as they don't bother you. (R6, FG1)

> I'm not at all racist. But there's a little bit of racism in every-
> body. (R8, FG1)

> I have two Algerian friends. I'm not a racist. (R1, FG2)

> I'm not racist at all. (R2, FG2)

> I'm not racist or anything but at the same time I wouldn't in-
> vite them into me home. So that makes me slightly racist,
> doesn't it? (R3, FG2)

NON-NATIONALS AND CRIME

The evidence from both survey material as well as the richer
interview material (although drawn from necessarily less representative focus groups) identify a hostility to outsiders with
some "old-fashioned" elements such as concerns about threat
to health and safety but more predominantly, elements of modern racism. These include the exaggeration of cultural differences and concerns about perceived inequality of treatment
("they're getting too much, too easily") at the hands of the state
and other organisations. These patterns are echoed, with varying weights for old-fashioned and modern racist elements in
many Western countries. In the UK, as was noted in the previous chapter, tabloid newspapers like *The Sun* with large read-
erships, have associated asylum-seekers with disease as well as
terrorism. The stereotype of asylum-seekers as "Trojan horse
terrorists" was given a boost when police raids of alleged terrorist cells netted a number of asylum-seekers from Algeria

and in the course of one of these raids, a police officer was
killed, in early 2003. In the US, harsher treatment of immigrants
and new requirements for those from 25 countries (Arab or
Muslim countries in all but one case) to register with the authorities both reflect and exacerbate public fears about foreign-
born residents. In France, as in a number of other continental
countries, the concern about asylum-seekers and legal as well
as illegal immigrants, especially from North Africa and Eastern
Europe, tends to be focused around insecurity in general and
street crime in particular.

While a link between crime and asylum-seekers is made in
Ireland, the concern has not up to now been mainly around
street crime but on fraud; there is a widespread perception that
those who come to Ireland claiming asylum are fraudulent. As
Curry (2000) noted, in his analysis of views of a sample of city-
centre Dublin residents, a majority of survey respondents believed that those claiming to be legitimate refugees were in reality economic migrants and that economic migrants in turn
were here to "sponge" off a generous welfare system. Some
newspaper headlines chime closely with this view; "Floodgates
open as new army of poor swamp the country" (*Sunday World*,
May 1997) as well as "Crackdown on 2,000 'sponger' refugees"
(*Irish Independent*, June 1997). The presence of these "unde-
serving masses", it is widely assumed, must be responsible for
the overloading of services such as those providing housing and
medical maternity care.

In the *Irish Independent* (25 March 2003) Tom Brady, the Security Editor, reported that the government was planning to in-
troduce finger-printing for most foreign nationals, including
"students, those with work permits, and the non-national parents
of Irish-born children".[19] The purpose of this procedure was "to
eliminate massive financial scams" ("mainly of the social welfare system", Brady added on a radio interview that day) and
the main problems "relate to Nigerians and Chinese". Finger-
printing had already been introduced for asylum-seekers and
was reported to be a "significant aid in cracking down on multi-

---

[19] Incidentally, the term "Irish-born children" makes an interesting distinction
to say, "Irish children".

ple applications for refugee status". The story appears to legitimise popular beliefs about the involvement of non-nationals in fraudulent crime. It was published on the front page of the *Irish Independent* with the headline, in large type, "Foreigners living here will be fingerprinted 'to stop scams'". The story was also covered on RTE Radio 1's flagship morning news programme, "Morning Ireland". In the course of the interview, David Hanly, the interviewer changed the focus of his questioning to a story Tom Brady had written a few days previously ("One in five sent to prison non-nationals, study shows", 19 March 2003).

> DH: And is it also the case that non-nationals make up 18 per cent of the Irish prison population right now?
>
> TB: Yeah, almost 1 in 5, according to figures we published last week . . .
>
> DH: And we have 10,000 prison inmates, or we did have in 2001? . . . Seventeen hundred of these were non-nationals,[20] from ninety countries?
>
> TB: Yeah, more than ninety countries were represented.

The *Irish Independent* and "Morning Ireland" have large audiences and for many people listening and reading, there appeared to be evidence that foreigners in Ireland were prone to crime, especially scams and fraud on the social welfare system. The issue of crime and non-nationals will be pursued in greater depth in Chapter Five.

In Chapter One, the various countries of origin of those seeking asylum in Ireland for 2001 were noted. It was also noted in Figure 1.1 that Nigerians, Romanians, Congolese and Algerians were the predominant nationalities of asylum-seekers into Ireland in the 1997–2001 period. To the casual observer, the numbers game may appear to support some loosely expressed

---

[20] This may have inadvertently misled the listener. In the discussion about finger-printing, "non-nationals" referred to those from outside the EU, Switzerland, Iceland and Liechtenstein. However, in the prison population statistics, "non-nationals" referred to anyone from outside Ireland. Thus the 1,700 inmates referred to by David Hanly included 225 from the UK and 64 from EU countries other than Ireland and the UK.

concerns that Ireland has become an "easy number" (or the "story had spread") among some nationalities such as Romanians and Nigerians. This issue will be taken up in Chapter Five.

PREDICTING THE FUTURE

To return to the question posed earlier in this chapter (and implicitly throughout this book): what are the prospects for Irish populism? If it is assumed that the European pattern will be at least partially reproduced in Ireland, then the likelihood in the medium term (within ten years) of populism having a significant impact on the political system must be high. Or phrasing it differently, it would be very surprising if right-wing populism did not make a substantial mark on Irish politics in the next few years. Why do I argue this? First, Irish society has experienced a whirlwind of change in the last two decades. Where right-wing populism attaches itself to a nostalgia for the old and critiques the excesses of the new, it is likely to win converts. Second, the direction of change favours the kinds of politics and the kinds of beliefs highlighted in Chapter Three. There is a growing scepticism about Europe, although from a low base. There is also a widespread, if not yet prevalent feeling, apparent from the two Nice Treaty referenda, that Brussels is dominating small countries like Ireland. And this growing Euro-scepticism has still to feel the benefit of a shift in European politics towards central and Eastern Europe as poorer applicant states join and are perceived to be taking Ireland's role as a deserving periphery. Thirdly, immigrants will become an ever-more integral part of Irish society and economic life. This process will be accelerated when citizens from ten accession states are given rights to live and work here from May 2004 following the signing of the Accession Treaties in April 2004. While it is likely that this will enhance Irish life, sections of the society will feel increasingly resentful about this gradual but powerful transformation. Most relevant still is the sense of grievance towards asylum-seekers in Ireland. Asylum-seekers appear to have become a focal point for the hostilities felt by many of the less well-off towards ethnic minorities, foreigners and outsiders in general. The speed of attitudinal change in this regard is phenomenal and in four to five years, the "aver-

age" perspective (which of course conceals both very favourable as well as distinctly hostile views) has altered from a typically non-populist one to one which places Ireland in among
those countries which have experienced sweeping populist inroads. With the exception of Luxembourg, every other country
experiencing the same intake of asylum-seekers has followed to
some extent the populist route. (This analysis incidentally does
not support the claim that racism is *caused* by the presence of
asylum-seekers; the ability of academics, experts as well as the
general public to get themselves in a twist over cause, blame
and association is virtually limitless — in the summary to this
chapter and in Chapter Five, the notion of cause will be teased
out further.) We have also seen, from survey evidence, plausibly
fleshed out by focus group material, that aside from concerns
about the numbers of asylum-seekers, there is a widespread
cynicism about the legitimacy of the claims made, particularly by
the "usual suspects", i.e. from certain countries, as well as their
supposed criminality, especially in the area of social welfare
fraud. These beliefs too will drawn upon by populist politics.

How might popular sentiment and resentment in Ireland become transformed into a political force? This is very difficult to
answer. As noted in the previous chapter, the leadership of
right-wing populist parties has often been taken by maverick,
politically astute, media-friendly figures. Such people are
harder to find than one might think. In current Irish political life
for example, it is probably fair to say that only a minority of figures have any real kind of charisma, public appeal or flair. For
every one skilled political spokesperson, there are several
gauche backwoodsmen who would make laughing stocks of
their parties were they propelled into the limelight (and most of
them have the good grace to know this). Thus leadership quali-
ties are not a given and the human factor in politics is always
important. This makes short- to medium-term predictions about
political change, even where one feels confident about the direction of the broader socio-economic trends, precarious; it also
makes fools of the predictors. But here are a few ways in which
patterns elsewhere in Europe might be extrapolated to Ireland:

- **Innovation** (the Danish/Dutch model): this is the breakthrough model where a radical right-wing populist party
  rocks the political equilibrium with a sudden and unexpected breakthrough, similar to the LPF in the Netherlands
  (see Chapter Three). An equivalent happening in Ireland
  might see the anti-immigrationist grouping, the Immigration
  Control Platform (ICP) take a number of seats in the local
  elections followed by a breakthrough into national politics in
  a general election. In its favour is the Irish electoral system,
  friendly to new, small political parties. In the 1997 general
  election, an ICP candidate took 0.84 per cent of the vote (293
  first preferences) in Cork South West (a three-seater), only
  0.03 of a quota necessary for election and came in eighth of
  nine candidates. In the 2002 general election, the candidate
  (Ní Chonaill) moved to a five-seat constituency, Dublin South
  Central (a surprising choice given that it is a relatively middle-class constituency), and took 2.10 per cent of the vote
  (926 first preferences) and 0.13 per cent of a quota, running
  in twelfth of fifteen candidates. The support is still small and
  this is not yet a breakthrough; but the ICP with only patchy
  canvassing and little evidence of postering or extensive leaf-
  leting, out-polled parties on the far left with greater community presence such as the Workers Party and the Socialist
  Workers Party. Against its possible breakthrough in Ireland
  is its lack of appeal to the middle classes, who tend to pre-
  dominate in the leadership of political parties. And its public
  spokesperson, Áine Ní Chonaill, is not overburdened with
  charisma.

- **Transformation** (the Swiss model): in this scenario, a significant but minor political party which finds itself becoming
  redundant, through say social and economic change, under-
  goes a change of leadership which tries to make the party
  relevant again by taking up populist policies, such as happened to the previously agrarian SVP in Switzerland. While
  Fine Gael's recent election disaster, leadership contest and
  subsequent process of profound navel-gazing superficially
  matches these criteria (although of course, Fine Gael is, or at
  least was, more than a minor player in an Irish context),

there is probably still too much of the social-democratic, Garret FitzGerald, liberal tradition in the party for this to occur, for the moment. It also has proven itself very pro-Europe and increasingly relies for its core vote among rural areas where migration issues are less potent (but could a right-wing populist identity relaunch its urban potential?)

Sinn Féin in the context of a post-armed-struggle Ireland, might more plausibly find a need to redefine itself. While this looks impossible under the current Northern leadership, political authority changes to fit new times. A Dublin-based leadership might find a radical anti-immigrant nationalist-populism playing well on the doorsteps. Against that likelihood are the historical leftist and anti-fascist (anti-Blueshirt) traditions of Irish republicanism, especially from the 1930s as well as their current anti-"big-capital" posturing.

The Progressive Democrats are a middle-class party to their very marrow; in Chapter Two, it was argued that the middle class do not have an inherent material interest in anti-immigrationism. Thus (and despite the surprising authoritarianism of the current PD Minister for Justice around issues of crime, journalist–Garda relations, and alcohol), they are unlikely to be in the running for the right-wing populist vote.

- **Absorption** (the UK model): this represents a model of how populism might fail to build an independent identity. Just as it has been proposed (and apparently fervently believed among the British far right) that the move to the right by Thatcher and the Conservative Party especially on immigration in the late 1970s thwarted the success of the National Front, it might be that the prevailing political forces in Ireland will move rightwards to head off the political appeal of a more radical grouping. In an Irish context, Fianna Fáil often calls itself the *populist party* of Ireland; some of its TDs might be happy to refer to themselves as the *right-wing populist party* and make appeals on policies further to the right than heretofore.

- **The Split**: although no clear case of success can be offered for this, a plausible scenario might involve segments or lay-ers of one or several establishment parties becoming increasingly dissatisfied with the radicalism of the party position on an issue like Europe, asylum-seekers or immigration. Party representatives could be expelled for their position and go back to the people, presenting themselves as courageous and honest underdogs, with a new populist political programme. Within Fianna Fáil, the case of Noel O'Flynn is interesting. In 1997, he barely made it as a successful election candidate, taking 11.23 per cent of the vote in his constituency (Cork North Central) and coming in third of the Fianna Fáil TDs. Between then and the 2002 election, he made a number of comments critical of "sponging" asylum-seekers. In 2002 he topped the poll (16.36 per cent of the vote) and was the first candidate elected in his constituency. What lessons will he and his colleagues have learned from this? Fianna Fáil's very size and aspiration to be an all-class, all-issue party make party discipline and unity more difficult to achieve. Indeed many of the current *soi-disant* independent TDs are, as one journalist noted, from the Fianna Fáil gene pool. It is far from inconceivable that a number of Fianna Fáil political candidates, in the run-up to an election, could seek to "play the race card" in their campaigns, lose the party whip but subsequently remain as *de facto* Fianna Fáil supporters (but nominal independents).

IN SUMMARY

The central prediction in this chapter is that right-wing populist politics will emerge as an important force in Ireland in the short- to medium-term future and perhaps as early as the local and European elections in June 2004. Background factors such as the decline of the Church (see Chapter One), growing Euro-scepticism (again, see Chapter One) and economic decline will play a role. However, the major force is likely to be hostility towards immigrants and refugees in Irish society, intertwined with different forms of racism. This argument is based simply on the fact that similar demographic shifts have been accompanied by such political changes in every other European society. There is no particular reason to hope that Irish civic beliefs, humanity and tolerance are rooted more deeply than in these other countries (and in many cases, frankly, one might guess that the roots of such Irish values are far more shallow). Does this mean that right-wing populism is likely to grow *because* of the numbers of newcomers to the society? Not at all. It does mean, however, that as minorities inevitably become more visible, they may become convenient scapegoats for many of the real and intractable problems faced especially by the disadvantaged in Irish society.

This chapter concluded by trying to offer some permutations as to how professional politicians might respond to a groundswell of attitudinal change among sections of the public. While the majority of Irish politicians have heretofore been reasonably principled, it is very difficult to imagine, in the cut-and-thrust of a subsequent election campaign, a substantial number not exploiting and manipulating public fear, misunderstanding and indeed envy towards immigrants and asylum-seekers and their perceived comforts. It may be too easy and ready a vote-winner for some to resist, particularly given the current embattled status of the governing and other parties. Imagine an election with Fianna Fáil TDs facing an angry public over economic downturn, or Sinn Féin politicians seeking to extend their support in deprived areas of Dublin or an Independent candidate who needs a bit of publicity to boost a campaign . . . Who would be strong enough to resist the race card then? And how many voters would be drawn towards it?

Chapter 5

WHAT IS TO BE DONE?

A SOCRATIC DEBATE

The conclusion of the previous chapter was that right-wing populism was likely to make a significant impact on Irish politics within the next ten years. So the obvious question is what, if anything, might be done to prevent this? Actually, this is only *one* obvious question since it assumes the answers to other questions such as why anything should be done, or even what we mean when we say "something should be done". I will try to answer the "obvious" question as well as other related ones by listing ten statements either in favour of, or resigned to, the progress of populism and then attempting to respond to and refute these statements. These statements are in no necessary order of importance although are loosely arranged from broader, more abstract ideas to more concrete, specific ones.

Argument 1: **Right-wing populism is a response to post-industrial uncertainty; thus, there are no policies at the level of the state that can deal with change at such a broad or global level.**

Refutation: This argument — that populist politics are a function of post-modernisation — was touched upon in Chapter Four in the description of Betz's (1994) analysis of radical right-wing populism in Europe. It is a coherent position but has trouble explaining the uneven successes of populism in various countries (since it is not clear that the more "post-industrialised" ones are necessarily more populist). It is also unsatisfactory that similar conclusions about the impact of the prevailing economic system have been reached before in a very different era and set of circumstances, e.g. such as when Hannah Arendt argued that capitalism was "post-modern" in the 1920s. It seems that capitalism is chronically post-modern! No doubt it consistently breaks up the old order — but it has been doing so for some time now, between two to three centuries, depending on perspective. We need to be clear about why and how capitalism's current activities are generating populist responses in Europe at this specific time. One also needs to be wary about terms like post-industrialisation and globalisation — they carry a good deal of baggage with lots of vagueness crammed into that baggage. And does "globalisation" represent the end of the old order or the foundations of the new? The trouble with such vagueness is that one cannot apply the normal criterion of falsifiability (i.e. the characteristics of being properly testable) to these claims or theories, as the philosopher Popper cogently argued one should be able to do. In Argument 9 below, a more concrete version of the post-industrial/post-modern position will be assessed and until then, left to one side.

Argument 2: **Populism is in part a response of frustration to an undemocratically administered EU and policy at the state level cannot effectively challenge the Brussels élite.**

Refutation: One of the problems in even raising an issue like EU administration is that readers can find themselves drifting off into a daydream until the next paragraph ambles along. However, despite its somnambulistic potential, the EU should demand our attention. It is an (increasingly) important institution in the lives of hundreds of millions. One does not have to be a dogged Euro-sceptic to be concerned about the democratic deficit in the running of Europe; even the "Yes" sides during the Nice Treaty referenda 1 and 2 quietly acknowledged problems in this regard. Will Hutton, author of the influential *The World We're In* (2002), is keenly in favour of the broad European project, partly as a counterweight to the increasingly one-dimensional free-market rightism of Washington. However, he recognises serious problems with the structure of current European governance. Even if it can convince people of its economic viability, the EU must refute "the charge that [it] is incapable of being democratic. Solve this and the only arguments left for the sceptics are prejudice and nostalgia" (2002: 346). The problem is that this is not an easy charge to refute. "Across the EU opinion polls show mounting scepticism about the European project, distrust of European initiatives and concern about the euro" (p. 348). The Swedish people rejected the euro by referendum in September 2003, partly through scepticism about the equal treatment of smaller nations within the EU (specifically in terms of the Stability Pact) and also through a perceived gap between the views of the political élite and the public. Particularly damaging to popular trust more broadly among EU publics was the report in March 1999 of the European Parliament which alleged that fraud and corruption in the EU Commission frequently pass unnoticed. The Parliament also noted that there was an absence of clear responsibility for the activities of the Commission. The entire top layer of officers of the Commission resigned after this devastating report. Hutton also points out that there are structural, not cosmetic problems with the running of the Commission and an ambiguity at its core. On the one hand, it is expected to serve, in a traditional civil servant role, the Council of Ministers. On the other hand, it is also expected to be an active innovator in European affairs and thus to direct, not simply serve the politicians. "It is at once the builder of a federal Europe and the custodian of a federation of nation-states" (p. 347). Another ambiguity is the manner in which European elections are used to create a European Parliament and yet they continue to be fought over national issues rather than those within a European public realm.

Hutton provides some sensible suggestions for revitalising European democracy. Before looking at those, it might be argued that regardless of their value, it is pointless for a small state like Ireland to hope to effect policy change at the EU. However, this is a weak argument; the aspiration across Europe is for more accountability in decision-making and persistent and consistent demands for movement in this direction will be difficult to overlook. Furthermore, if Irish representatives in Europe are seen to be actively and genuinely pursuing a democratic agenda rather than one that strenuously seeks to avoid rocking the boat, this will sap the political appeal of Euro-scepticism in Ireland. For what kind of changes might one argue?

Hutton proposes a reinvigoration of European institutions. At the core is a struggle for legitimacy and a requirement that the European Parliament needs to be at the heart of European democracy. There is a chicken-and-egg problem here: for "Europe" to work, a European consciousness must develop whereby people think in European terms. Pan-European institutions then become invested with more meaning and legitimacy. But currently, it is national governments and parliaments that enjoy (generally declining) authority and legitimacy. Hutton suggests that we must be realistic about integration; a "genuine European civil society, a Europe-wide public sphere and a common political culture" do not currently exist and will not spring up overnight. Therefore, the process will take time and needs careful but also radical change to support its development. Hutton proposes more regular meetings for the European Council of heads of government. Other potential reforms proposed include the direct election of the president of the Commission by the citizens of Europe. The rotation between member states of the headship of the Council of Europe should be abandoned and replaced by a permanent council made up of a Minister for Europe from each member state and chaired by the president of the Commission. Directives emanating from this Council should be approved not just by the European Parliament but also by a European senate composed of delegates from each national parliament. Areas of decision-making for national governments, such as in health, education, law and order, and welfare should be clearly defined and ring-fenced to allay the fears of those concerned with the usurping of rights of the nation-state. The implementation of these changes is not far-fetched; the reforms are typical of those under consideration in plans for an EU constitution. A draft constitution drawn up by a convention presided over by Valéry Giscard d'Estaing will be examined by an Inter-Governmental Conference commencing in October 2003. This constitution, if accepted, would give the EU a formal legal personality, a bill of rights and (obviously) a constitution all for the first time. Ultimately though, the European Parliament will have to be given more core power, especially over taxation, since citizens quickly engage with an institution when it has tax-altering powers; even the draft constitution's hints at change in this area (e.g. towards majority voting on the harmonisation of corporation tax) will certainly be rejected by the British, Spanish and Irish governments.

One may quibble with many of Hutton's suggestions or those of other reformers. The thrust of these arguments, though, that decision-making in the EU must operate with a high level of public scrutiny and be accountable, is surely the important principle. One of the main themes of the populist right is that Brussels is operated by cynical, anti-democratic and élitist fixing. If established political parties are seen to be genuinely committed, as opposed to paying lip service, to the principle of expanding democracy and accountability within the EU, this kicks away one of the key buttresses of the populists.

Argument 3: Right-wing populism is based on hostility to outsiders and both history and psychology demonstrate that this hostility is widespread and inevitable (or, "The Tragic Vision, Part 1").

Refutation: Steven Pinker, in his influential book *The Blank Slate*, has argued that there are two conflicting visions of the nature of human beings, the Tragic and the Utopian (or what Thomas Sowell, 1987, has called the Constrained and Unconstrained). The Utopian vision is associated with Rousseau, Condorcet, Paine, Galbraith and Marx and it holds that humans' "psychological limitations are artefacts that *come from* our social arrangements" (Pinker, 2002; 287). If we change society, human nature itself will change. The Tragic vision, associated with Burke, Hobbes, Smith, Popper, Hayek (and actually Marx again), however, perceives humans as inherently limited in their thinking and ultimately selfish to the core. For proponents of the Tragic vision, the validity of pessimism about human nature is confirmed by studies demonstrating: the primacy of family ties and nepotism in human societies, the poor record humans have in sharing communal goods and the universality of violence in all human societies. Social psychologists have revealed that humans have an automatic tendency to categorise people into in- and out-groups and to be positively biased towards their own group (see Tajfel, 1981 and Sherif, 1966). Pinker tends to favour the Tragic vision of humanity; he approvingly quotes Adam Smith's illustration of the human tendency towards bias in favour of our in-group and indifference or hostility to outsiders. Smith had hypothetically asked how a European might respond to the news that all of China had been swallowed up in an earthquake.

> He would, I imagine, first of all express very strongly his sorrow for the misfortune of that unhappy people, he would make many melancholy reflections upon the precariousness of human life, and the vanity of all the labours of man. . . . And when all this fine philosophy was over, when all these humane sentiments had been once fairly expressed, he would pursue his business or pleasure, take his repose or his diversion, with the same ease and tranquillity as if no such accident had happened. . . . If he was to lose his little finger tomorrow, he would not sleep tonight; but provided he never saw them, he would snore with the most profound security over the ruin of a hundred million of his brethren. (Smith, 1759; quoted in Pinker, p. 288)

If xenophobia and in-group bias are inherent in human beings, is there any defence against a political current seeking to exploit them? There are two responses to the Tragic Vision. The first is that people are not exclusively amoral; historical evidence confirms that humans have always been able to show sympathy for other humans while also apparently able to commit atrocities against others still. Pinker argues that this apparent paradox exists because human beings have devised a moral circle embracing members of their clan, family or tribe. "Inside the circle, fellow humans are targets of sympathy; outside they are treated like a rock or a river or a lump of food" (p. 320). The process of civilisation, it follows, essentially means reducing the number of humans outside the circle (those you can kill and eat)[21] and increasing those inside the circle, to whom one should show sym-

---

[21] This includes other human beings. Pinker argues that the prevalence of cannibalism in human societies has been understated.

pathy. The good news is that, over millennia, civilisation, as defined by this criterion, is growing and our vision of the human need not be quite so Tragic. (Incidentally, in a more mundane context, the need to draw minorities into the inner circle makes clear how important it is to have minority representation in popular television shows such as soaps. Their inclusion means that viewers get involved with their stories so they become humanised; the feeling of sympathy for a character widens the circle around them.) Furthermore, the fair or humane treatment of people from other countries and ethnic groups does not have to rely purely on altruism and utopianism; as we will see below, there may be reasonable arguments grounded in self-interest for rejecting xenophobic, other-resenting politics.

Argument 4: **People are ultimately selfish and since right-wing populism bases itself on human selfishness, it is impossible to resist (or, "The Tragic Vision, Part 2").**

Refutation: People are naturally self-centred, it might be reasonably asserted. In larger groups, they favour their own and since they see no personal benefit in helping out others, they may have an automatic hostility to outsiders such as immigrants and asylum-seekers. So, even if one could show that, on average, a typical non-national, say, committed half the crimes of a national, someone might argue that even one crime is one too many among non-nationals — why should we have to endure any at all? The debate about whether people are always self-centred or can at times be altruistic is a complex one within social psychology and one that cannot be pursued here. (See Batson, 1995, for a sophisticated position sympathetic to the idea that some people sometimes show genuine altruism to some other people.) Whether or not real altruism exists (behaviour carried out which is motivated primarily by concern for the welfare of others), it is clear that pro-social behaviour certainly does and people often carry out actions that benefit others, even if their motivation is ultimately egoistic. For example, we have seen evidence in Chapter Three that most people are uncomfortable with accusations of racism. Thus they may be willing to make at least small sacrifices in order not to be accused of being xenophobic. In fact, they are threatened with cognitive dissonance — the contradiction between different beliefs — if they hold a view of themselves as non-prejudiced and then act in a prejudiced fashion. Furthermore, the existence of recipro-cal altruism is uncontested among psychologists — this is the idea that people help others in the expectation that they will be given help in turn if they need it. It is clear therefore that the no-tion of human beings as purely driven by short-term cost–benefit calculations is absurd and they are willing, at least in some circumstances, to trade short-term assets for long-term benefits. Thus, it is likely that most Irish people are willing to "tolerate" asylum-seekers in return for a national reputation of humaneness and openness. Despite growing secularisation, Christian belief and ideology cannot disappear overnight and at some level, people have to square their rhetoric and behaviour.

But we can go further. So far, we have been thinking about the presence of non-nationals as something to be grudgingly tolerated. In fact, most non-nationals living in Ireland are legal immigrants, working and contributing to the economy and benefiting the Irish population as a whole (see Chapter Two also). As *The Economist* noted:

> . . . the movement of humanity brings undoubted gains, and not just to the immigrants. . . the potential economic benefits to the world of liberalising migration dwarf those from re-moving trade barriers . . . Immigrants, unlike natives, move readily to areas where labour is in short supply, so easing bottlenecks. They bring a just-in-time supply of skills, too. . . . In many cases, immigrants also pay more in taxes than they cost in public spending. (Leader article, 2 November 2002)

So one can be as self-centred as one likes and still reject the populist hostility to foreigners. The announcement by the De-partment of Trade and Enterprise in March/April 2003 that it was reducing the number of one-year employment visas available for different groups of non-national workers was met with wide-spread alarm, especially among employers, rather than relief. Furthermore, in ageing Europe, the population is no longer re-producing itself. As Ringen (2003) has pointed out, by 2050, the European population is expected to be 600 million, down from

750 million at the turn of the millennium. The self-interest of EU states — in fact their very survival in the long-term — certainly lies with attracting workers from elsewhere to migrate. (It might also be worthwhile, Ringen suggests, trying to make European societies more attractive places for people to have children.)

***Argument 5:* Irish people need not feel guilty about adopting populist politics since Ireland never had an empire and doesn't "owe anything" to less developed countries.**

Refutation: This curious argument occasionally pops up in the letters pages of national newspapers and holds that, while the generally larger states of Europe, with their histories of empire, should be guilty about expressing racism and anti-immigrant politics, the same is not true of Ireland. Strictly speaking, Ireland was very much part of the British Empire during the "scramble for Africa" and rampant European colonialism of the late nineteenth century. Even if it is protested that Ireland was a colonised country that happened to be in Europe, rather than a coloniser of people elsewhere, the pattern of twentieth-century emigration cannot be overlooked. Ireland's faltering economy meant that migrant workers left Ireland for elsewhere, in huge numbers and often working illegally, from the earliest years of the "Free State" until the early 1990s. If reciprocation requires an earlier debt, then it is clear that in the emigration stakes, if less so in the empire ones, Ireland owes. And more profoundly, what kind of state and what kind of people only permit themselves to engage in humane behaviour towards those experiencing wretched conditions elsewhere when it's "owed"?

***Argument 6:* Populist policies should be supported, not challenged. They are rational and fair-minded responses to the current situation where Ireland has (a) too many asylum-seekers for a small country, (b) of whom too many are not genuine, (c) who are here to simply and fraudulently enjoy a cushy existence and (d) engage in serious amounts of crime.**

Refutation: And this, to a large degree, is the nub of it. What if the problem with populist politics is that they've got it right?

Peter Mandelson commented in the UK context that "progressives have got to come to terms with right-wing populism".
Does this mean co-opting its policies? In January 2003, the Supreme Court refused the appeal of non-national parents of Irish
citizens against deportation. Was this an example of the authorities coming to terms with right-wing populism? While the legal
bases for such a decision must be complex, it is interesting that
the summary of the comments of Mr Justice Adrian Hardiman,
one of those who rejected the appeal, included the argument
that the "common good can include consideration of the statistical pattern of immigration and asylum-seeking" (summary
compiled by Carol Coulter, *Irish Times*, 24 January 2003, p. 8).
On the front page of that newspaper on the same date, the
background to the Supreme Court decision included "concerns
that the refugee system was being abused". Furthermore, in
July 2002, the Gardaí launched Operation Hyphen, a "huge
show of force, aimed allegedly at illegal immigrants" (Fintan
O'Toole, *Irish Times*, 29 October 2002, p. 4) in the Dublin region. O'Toole suggests that the operation, in which 140 people
were arrested (of whom only 16 were evading deportation or-
ders) to pursue illegal immigrants was "a gesture of appease-
ment to the far right . . . in effect if not intent, a piece of anti-
immigrant propaganda". Again, this offers an example of the
authorities getting "tough" on immigrants and asylum-seekers;
it seems to suggest then that some of the public concerns about
the numbers and legitimacy of asylum-seekers are justified. Let
us look at the validity of the claims made above in Argument 6.

*Argument 6(a): The numbers of asylum-seekers in Ireland are too
great*

Refutation: The numbers of asylum-seekers in the European Union have declined from 675,455 in 1992 to 388,372 in 2002 — i.e.
almost halved (annex c.2, p. 113, the UNHCR Statistical Yearbook 2001). (The National Consultative Committee on Racism
and Interculturalism has suggested that, as internal borders
within the EU are relaxed, external borders are being tightened
through greater restrictions, including the use of lists of countries by some EU states from whom they will not accept refugees

and more stringent procedures for assessing asylum-seekers. This has led to a sharp decline in those seeking asylum in countries like Germany. See www.nccri.com/refugees.html.) This means that of the world's estimated 20 million refugees, less than 5 per cent now make it to Europe to apply for asylum. Tanzania, with its 35 million population and annual average per capita income equivalent to several hundred euro, offered refuge to 498,000 asylum-seekers and 300,000 displaced Burundians in 2001 (US Committee for Refugees, see www.refugees.org), the combined figure of 798,000 close to the 972,800 offered by *all* European (EU and non-EU) states in that year. Between 1992 and 2001, Ireland had 39,749 new asylum applications, just over 1 per cent of all EU applications. This number, over a ten-year period, is substantially less than the population of county Carlow, one of Ireland's less populated counties, or about one-fifth of the population of Dun Laoghaire-Rathdown. The number of Irish asylum-applications from Nigerian citizens, as noted in the previous chapter, was 11,154 for the years 1997–2001. This "influx" represents less than one ten-thousandth of the Nigerian population (in 2001). This figure for a five-year period is also, in raw numbers, about one quarter of the numbers of net outward economic Irish migrants who, on an *annual* basis, exported themselves to other countries, in the 1950s; this line of argument of course only holds if one wants to adopt the "who owes"? perspective. And finally, with regard to the numbers game, what about the dog that didn't bark? Ireland, for example, only received 68 asylum applications from Turkey between 1997 and 2001, while in that period, 133,604 people from Turkey sought asylum, mainly in other EU countries. And only 60 Afghans sought refuge in Ireland out of an entire total of 143,766 from that troubled country seeking refuge in the 1997–2001 period. The state is far from being "overrun" by asylum-seekers.

Argument 6(b): The asylum-seekers who are here are mainly bogus

Refutation: It was noted in Chapter One (see Figure 1.1) that Nigeria, Romania, the Democratic Republic of Congo and Algeria were the countries from which asylum-seekers to Ireland most commonly came from 1997 to 2001. Refugees are accepted as genuine where they have a well-founded fear of persecution on the grounds of race, religion, nationality or membership of a particular social or political group. How well-founded a fear of persecution might people have had in the four states named above between 1997 and 2001?

Nigeria was under military rule until May 1999 and was the pariah of Africa for the brutality shown towards dissidents and minority groups. Its execution of writer Ken Saro-Wiwa in 1995 shocked many. Even the return to "supposedly democratic politics" (*The Economist*, 13 September 2001) has not made life much easier for many of its 120 million people. Politicians seek support often by playing on rivalries between different ethnic groupings; the results have been disastrous. Between May 1999 and September 2001, over 6,000 people died in communal violence. In one week in September 2001, 500 people were killed and 900 injured in clashes of rival ethnic groups in the city of Jos. In June and July of that year, 200 people died in the state of Nasarawa. Strife between Muslims and Christians is also common and led to 2,000 deaths following clashes in Kaduna in February 2000. Rather than providing a neutral force buffering the mainly Muslim north and mainly Christian south, the army is "increasingly out of control" (*Economist*, 1 November 2001) and was accused of carrying out a policy of revenge in slaughtering 300 villagers in the state of Benue in October 2001. Even the return to democracy in the national presidential elections of April 2003 has been clouded in killings and serious allegations of vote-rigging.

The Amnesty International report on Romania documents many cases of torture and ill-treatment by the police in order to obtain confessions. Unlawful use of firearms by the police are also widely reported, including a large-scale indiscriminate "revenge" attack by several hundred special police officers on a village of 1,300 people. Racist attacks and police ill-treatment of detainees are also widespread. Pogroms and attacks on Roma (gypsies) are also well-documented and have been highlighted by the EU as a major obstacle to Romania's accession to the EU.

Algeria's eight-year civil war has been gruesome by any standards — a measure of its cruelty was that the death of 800 people in the first six months of 2002 was regarded as a diminution of the previous intensity. The machine-gunning of 13 passengers on a suburban bus in the small town of Larba in June 2002 failed to make any impact on the international media. Although elections are held, "with all the trappings of a democracy, the country remains a thinly veiled military dictatorship" (*Economist*, 11 July 2002). The Berber-speaking region has witnessed massive protests at the level of government repression in Kabylia.

The Democratic Republic of Congo (formerly Zaïre) must be the most tragic of the four countries. Mobuto, the country's dictator, was toppled in 1994 but the intervening period has not seen the emergence of a democratic Congo. Rather, a dozen mini-wars overlap, including a civil war and the intervention of the armies or backed-militias of five neighbouring or nearby states, Angola, Uganda, Zimbabwe, Rwanda and Burundi. Some of the Hutu-Tutsi tensions that led to the holocaust of Tutsis in Rwanda are being replayed in Congo, although some of the fiercest fighting has also occurred between the Tutsi-dominated Rwandan army and Congolese Tutsis. In probably the world's bloodiest and least reported set of wars, more than three million people are estimated to have been killed (this figure is certainly conservative; in an *Observer* article on 13 April 2003, 4.7 million was the guesstimate of the number of deaths). The use of torture, rape and amputation of limbs as terror policies are widespread. Amnesty annual reports are normally about one or two pages long for any given country; in the case of Congo, the report runs to 19 pages. As so often in human history, the civil war components of the conflict are the most horrific; the normally sober *Economist* reports that a rebel group in the town of Kisangani slaughtered 150 people on 14 May 2002, "then pitched their disembowelled bodies into the river with stones crammed into their bellies" ("Africa's Great War", 4 July 2002).

One might consider by comparison the heartbreak and anguish that the violence in Northern Ireland has caused over its three decades. Yet it is clear that in the context of the standards of human misery in recent years among the countries high-

lighted above, Northern Ireland in the worst of times looks almost normal. Thus, given the turmoil of those countries from
where the largest numbers of asylum-seekers to Ireland origi-
nate, why is it so difficult to believe that many have "well-
founded" fears of persecution or worse? And why are we so
ready to assume they must be bogus, as seems implicit in the
front-page headline of the *Wexford People* in August 1998,
"Refugees: It's time to end the fiasco"? (An analysis of the survival rates of those asylum-seekers returned from the EU, or
indeed the US, to their own societies might be chilling.)

One reason indirectly alluded to in the media is the failure
of some asylum-seekers in Ireland to attend the appeal against
refusals to grant asylum. ("One-in-four appeals over asylum are
never heard", *Irish Times*, 22 April 2003, p. 5). Over a two-year
period (2001–2002), the Refugee Appeals Tribunal found that 23
per cent of cases appealing a refusal to grant asylum by the
Refugee Applications Commissioner were "no-shows" or with-
drawals. Why not show up if your case is genuine? Well, a large
majority did (so by the logic of the detractors, a large majority
are automatically genuine). And the proportion of no-shows for
2002 alone was 18.6 per cent, less than one in five. Nor is the
appeal system, to its credit, a mere rubber stamp. A quarter of
those appealing were granted refugee status. (But why then did
they have to rely on an appeal?) Given these odds, why would a
cynical bogus claimant not turn up when there's nothing to
lose? On the other hand, those who are genuine but confused
by Irish bureaucracy, or exhausted by the process, or too trau-
matised and numbed, or fearful that an Irish appeal board will
not comprehend conditions in a society half a world away,
might be more likely to give up. In fact, numbness and apathy
are classic symptoms of trauma (see Pitman et al., 2000), not of
people on the make.

*Argument 6(c): Asylum-seekers enjoy and are attracted to the
cushy conditions prevailing in Ireland*

Refutation: Those asylum-seekers in Ireland who made their application prior to 26 July 1999 are entitled to look for work and to
unemployment assistance if they cannot find work. Thus, they

are entitled to no more or less than the average EU citizen
. . . except for the cultural and linguistic barriers as well as the
probable absence of recognised qualifications enabling them to
easily find employment as well as the racism and discrimination
they face daily (of course, some EU citizens in their own and
other countries will also experience this). Thus, the reality for
many will be surviving on the dole in a strange, often racist
country, not normally considered the cushiest of situations.
However, they are better off than those asylum-seekers who
made their applications between 26 July 1999 and 10 April 2000;
this group is not entitled to work while their application is being
assessed. They are entitled to receive Supplementary Welfare
Allowances, Child Benefit where applicable, a medical card,
and are entitled to rent allowance, but are *not allowed* to go on
local authority housing lists. However, the least cushy conditions
prevail for those who made their application since 10 April 2000.
The introduction of the Dispersal/Direct Provision (D/DP) policy
means that this group is not entitled to do paid work and not entitled to rent allowance. Instead, after a week or so in a recep-
tion centre in Dublin, they are dispersed to large centres
outside Dublin where they are accommodated, receive full
board, a medical card and €19.05 a week pocket money (plus
€9.52 per child). They are not allowed to leave the state, risking
possible jail if they try. The sum of money involved is hardly a
draw, since €19.05 might just about cover the costs of some-
body's smoking habit, if s/he had decided to seriously cut
down. So that's the entire cushy package for Ireland's asylum-
seekers (and this does not include the original cost of getting to
Ireland).

*Argument 6(d): Immigrants and asylum-seekers engage in
serious amounts of crime*

Refutation: In Chapter Four, the coverage of the issue of crime
and non-nationals was discussed. The claim that 18 per cent of
the inhabitants of Irish jails in 2001 were non-nationals was
mentioned. Unusually for a figure being bandied about on the
national media, it turns out that 18 per cent is actually accurate.
Thus there appears to have been an over-representation of non-

nationals in Irish jails in 2001. One could spend a good deal of
time with the technicalities of this statistic. How much time did
the 18 per cent of non-nationals actually spend in prison? How
many were there for trivial issues relating to delays in paper-
work, the kind that Fintan O'Toole noted was one consequence
of the Gardaí's Operation Hyphen? How many were in simply
for other offences relating to laws on immigration, or awaiting
deportation? Was 2001 an exceptional year? However, it is
probably more sensible to deal with the substantive issue. Why
are non-nationals statistically more likely to end up in courts
and prisons than nationals? If liberals don't ask and attempt to
answer the tough questions, then the far right will trumpet their
own answers. The statistics are very limited for the moment in
Ireland, but the European pattern is very clear. Tournier (1999)
has provided estimates of the proportion of foreign-born pris-
oners in European jails across many countries. In France, it is
26 per cent; in Austria, it is 27 per cent; in the Netherlands, 32
per cent; in Germany, 34 per cent; in Belgium, 38 per cent; and
in Greece, 39 per cent. These figures, in France for example,
do not include the "nationals perceived and treated as foreigners by the police and judicial apparatus, such as youth born to
North African immigrants" (Wacquant, 1999; 217). The crimi-
nologist Tonry has stated it baldly: "members of *some* disadvantaged minority groups in every Western country are
disproportionately likely to be arrested, convicted, and imprisoned for violent, property, and drug crimes" (1997; 1). The
trends involving incarceration of huge numbers of African-
Americans in the US are widely known. Heretofore, Travellers
in Ireland have received a disproportionate deal of the attention of the police and courts; in the future, it is possible that this
will be true for some non-national groups. How can the disproportionate involvement in the criminal justice system of some
minorities be explained?

First, there is the issue of what criminologists call the "animus" of the system, such as police racism. This undoubtedly
plays a role, along with the indifference of many police officers
to minority group victimisation (something the Lawrence In-
quiry in Britain exposed). However, detailed research such as
self-report and victimisation studies confirms that "most of the

measured disparity [between minority groups and general population] appears to be attributable to offending differences" rather than because of invidious bias (Tonry, 1997; 11), and the same is generally true of sentencing differences.

However, the popular attribution by non-immigrants of social problems such as crime to immigrants was not one shared in the past by researchers. It is widely asserted that "first-generation immigrants are typically more law-abiding that the resident population" (ibid.; 19). It was among the children and grandchildren of immigrants, experiencing assimilation problems, that high crime involvement was anticipated. The consensus that high crime was associated "not with the foreign born but their children" held true for American immigration, as well as that of Germany, France and Switzerland. However, this view is gradually being seen as overly simplistic — for example, economic migrants from many Asian countries have lower crime rates in first *and* subsequent generations. This may arise as a consequence of patterns of self-help and ethnic-group networks of economic activity. Swedish research into the reasons why people have come to another country also reveals some unexpected findings. The research looked at the experiences of guest workers from Croatia and Serbia migrating in the 1950s as well as more recent arrivals of refugees from these same countries. The older group showed the American pattern of law-abiding first generations. However those who arrived later, mainly as refugees, showed, among the first generation, higher levels of offending, victimisation, unemployment, welfare dependence and family break-up. Martens (1995) cites estimates that between 20 and 25 per cent of refugees from these countries to Sweden had experienced physical torture and many suffered from post-traumatic stress disorder. "Seeing a close relative being ill-treated, killed or arrested . . . are examples of mentally traumatic experiences that are common in refugees" (Angel and Hjern, 1992: 36). The effects of this trauma "include alienation, apathy, lack of trust in personal relationships, reduced ability to plan for the future, irritability, and exaggerated reactions to emotionally charged situations" (Tonry, 1997; 24). Along with the isolation and reduced self-esteem of being an asylum-seeker, these are all the factors which "increase the individual tendency to commit crime" (Martens, 1995; 287). In other words, this research should make us think again about simple dichotomies of good asylum-seeker versus bad economic migrant; it appears that the traumatic processes associated with becoming a refugee/asylum-seeker may contribute to the difficulty that an individual has in assimilating. "Real" refugees may be made socially dysfunctional by their experiences (just as the experience of "real" poverty within a society is one powerful predictor of criminal involvement).

Of course, economic and social disadvantage are also associated with higher crime and imprisonment rates. That was true of Irish emigrants to the UK or Finns to Sweden just as it is true of many black minority groups today. Economic and social disadvantage is among the strongest predictors of involvement in crime in any population. Apparently neutral legal practices also operate to the systematic disadvantage of minority groups. For example, a logical practice is for people, where possible, not to be incarcerated before their trial. Only those deemed unlikely to appear for trial are imprisoned. But it is those who live the least settled lives who are deemed less likely to appear and therefore more often are held in prison. And of course, the disadvantaged — disproportionately more likely to be from minority groups — live less settled lives in terms of permanent places of residence or fixed employment. Hood (1992) has also found that black defendants in the UK, because of alienation from the legal system, are less likely to plead guilty than whites, and thus if found guilty, fail to obtain court leniency (the guilty plea being thought to provide evidence of contrition and responsibility).

The overall picture of non-nationals and crime is thus complex. We have already seen that in some cases, first generations are less likely to be involved in crime than the resident population. Substantial differences between different minority groups should also be recognised. For example, in the UK, Afro-Caribbeans have far higher crime and imprisonment rates than whites, yet Bangladeshis, "on average poorer and more disadvantaged than Afro-Caribbeans . . . are less involved in crime and the justice system than are whites" (Tonry, 1997; 1–2). In the Netherlands, Turks and Moroccans came in large numbers as guest workers in the 1950s and 1960s. They and their families are still economically disadvantaged compared to the Dutch, yet Turkish crime and incarceration rates are only slightly higher than for the Dutch while they are substantially higher for the Moroccans. So cultural differences among different minority groups with apparently similar economic situations can make a substantial difference. The good news is that policy can make a difference also. Martens (1997), in the Swedish context, has pointed out that policies of the Swedish social welfare system, such as health checks on pregnant mothers, special needs teaching in schools as well as language training for children of immigrants, quality pre-schools and a "Headstart" type of programme to help disadvantaged children have contributed to keeping second-generation immigrant crime low.

Overall, it should not be surprising if the issue of crime and non-nationals crops up repeatedly in Ireland. Higher levels of offending by non-nationals, while far from inevitable (given generational and cultural differences) are possible, in the context of the economic and social disadvantage of many newcomers, as well as low self-esteem, alienation, cultural problems, possible trauma, the experience of racism and discrimination, as well as the systematic exacerbation of the situation caused by apparently neutral legal practices. An appreciation of the causes behind possible differences as well as an awareness that sensible governmental policy can make a big difference are important weapons to prevent the populist right from using crime as an election issue.

Argument 7: **Right-wing populism appeals to the irrational element in people's thinking. Since people aren't very rational, it's difficult to combat (or, "The Tragic Vision, Part 3").**

Refutation: The elements of the tragic vision outlined earlier under Arguments 3 and 4 claimed that, in general, people are fundamentally prone to selfishness and more specifically, in-group bias or ethnocentrism. The final component of the tragic vision crowns these elements with an ironic twist — this argues that human thought is flawed, so poor in fact that we don't even realise that we are prone to racism or selfishness. Cognitive psychologists have found that people employ all sorts of biases to maintain a feel-good mental reality. Thus, evidence shows that people rely on a powerful self-serving bias and overestimate their capability in many domains, ranging from intellectual power, to their physical looks, to their sociability. While being fairly shrewd judges of other people, we fall for all kinds of crass self-deceptions when the issue is "me". Virtually everyone believes that he or she is decent — in fact more decent than most others — and also wiser than others also. As Hobbes noted:

> for such is the nature of men, that howsoever they may ac-
> knowledge many others to be more witty, or more eloquent,
> or more learned: Yet they will hardly believe there be many
> so wise as themselves. (1651; 82).

This capacity for massive self-deception and a belief in our fundamental decency actually makes it more difficult to confront racism. For example, in a positive move, the Department of Justice, Equality and Law Reform launched a National Anti-Racism Awareness Programme in October 2001 called "Know Racism" which set out to "create conditions that make it difficult for racism to exist here". One element of this programme was to issue leaflets with a ten-point code to follow — this code included "treat[ing] people from minority groups with the same respect you show to other people" and "extend[ing] a hand of friendship to persons of different cultural backgrounds". However, there must be an element of preaching to the converted here — those who bother to read the code have probably already made up their mind about racism. Asking "what's to be done about racism?" presupposes the reader's support. And it is difficult to imagine people reading the leaflet deciding to henceforth change their behaviour. Most of us feel we are pretty decent anyway and don't need such persuasion. Those who do consciously hold racist attitudes must go through various rationalisations about their views (see Chapter Three for examples of this) and feel they are too "wised-up" for this sort of leaflet. (That's not to say that such leaflets are unimportant; in fact they send a useful signal about the views of the establishment.)

It is likely that many of us also hold unconsciously biased views. For example, there is evidence that people are chronic users of stereotypes, biased simplified evaluations of social groups. Humans do not process information in a disinterested or consistent way — for example, we share a tendency to assume that out-groups are "all the same" while (our) in-group is varied — "they all look alike, but we are diverse" (see Hogg and Vaughan, 2002). We often form inaccurate stereotypes of groups even when we have no first-hand experience of them. Because we can only overrule our stereotypes with conscious deliberate reasoning, or through direct experience with minority groups over time, they come especially into use when we are in pressure or stress situations and our limited cognitive resources for conscious deliberation have to be directed elsewhere. Humans also tend to perceive an "illusory correlation" based on paired associations. Since negative events are distinctive (because they are subjectively rarer) and since minority groups are distinctive because the majority tend to have fewer encounters with them, illusory correlation by association may occur when a member of a minority group does something negative. Howard and Rothbart (1980), for example have shown that we tend to remember when out-group members engage in unfavourable acts (e.g. crime) but far less when they engage in favourable ones and the bias is reversed for in-group members. Thus we can understand the power of the media in shaping negative attitudes to minorities. To run a larger number of positive rather than negative stories in the media about minorities may look objectively like it is neutral or even pro-minority. However, the media must be especially vigilant because it is likely that the negative stories will be remembered long after the positive ones are forgotten and through illusory correlation, an association made between the behaviour outlined and the minority group cited. One might still recall the infamous Willie Horton story where, in the run-up to a presidential election, a pro-republican US political action committee used the media to highlight the actions of a black murderer. Released under a "prison furlough programme", Horton carried out a brutal rape and assault, while Democratic presidential candidate Michael Dukakis was Governor of Massachusetts, the jurisdiction in which Horton had been imprisoned and released. A decision by an Irish tabloid, *The Star*, in June 1997 to use a headline: "Refugee Rapists on the Rampage" replayed the same themes, with alliteration adding the extra kick. A single evocative story involving violent or sexual crime and a black man may have more resonance and impact than ten thousand words carefully outlining the complex causation of crime.

However, one should not despair of human cognition entirely; we are capable of deliberative non-stereotypical thought. Although we tend to use short cuts or heuristics to get to answers quickly, systematic errors occur but are not inevitable. Most of us are aware that our thinking relies on stereotypes and that though these stereotypes are often right, they may also be wrong. Although we are influenced by the biased accounts of the world through the mass media, most of us understand that the media account is just that — an account — not a picture of an objective reality. Indeed, a good deal of the pessimism of an earlier cognitive psychology in which people were viewed as "cognitive misers" has been overturned and replaced with a model of people as "motivated tacticians", capable of using their mental resources usually in a rational way. Pairing or association of minority groups with positive and perhaps more importantly neutral stimuli, while weaker than negative association, does occur and mass media campaigns can add their weight to this process. (Carroll, 2003, found that media campaigns in Ireland using either "multi-cultural" or "colour-blind" perspectives, while not changing levels of stereotyping of minorities, could significantly reduce racism.) While language and linguistic terms influence us, fewer researchers now hold the strong constructionist position that language and its categories entirely structure our thinking.

Argument 8: **Right-wing populism is more common in countries with a strong social-democratic tradition; therefore the disbandment of social democracy is the best defence against it (or, "The Tragic Society, Part 1").**

Refutation: In Chapter Three, it was noted that some small wealthy European countries tend to be "stakeholder" societies — ones where all members are entitled to important social goods like free health at the point of delivery, say, in strong contrast to the US. There is nothing odd in the fact that these societies are likely to be more attractive to certain groups of immigrants and asylum-seekers (as no doubt are other factors like family links, linguistic similarity, cultural knowledge and indeed the general humaneness of a society). But it must be a *reductio ad absurdum* to argue that since certain aspects of a society are attractive and thus act as pull factors to outsiders, and since outsiders generate populism, the smartest thing to do is to abolish these attractive factors. In fact, Milton Friedman, the widely respected right-wing economist and founder of monetarism, in an interview in 1998, claimed that, "it's obvious you can't have immigration and a welfare state" (in the same interview, incidentally, he claimed that the euro would never happen and the stock market was not setting up for a major crash; Friedman, 1998). But, of course, there are push factors behind the widescale movement of people and far more than one pull factor. The idea of making our societies as uncomfortable as possible for its members is the logic of cutting off our nose to spite our faces. It also propels forward a battle of lowest-common-denominator where each state tries to do as little as possible for its citizens. In fact, it is to their credit that many small European states can both accept those seeking asylum, as well as immigrants looking to build a new life, and continue to provide basic guarantees to people on fronts such as health, education and housing. A widespread sense of social justice and inclusiveness are the ideological foundations for social democracy *and* for resisting populist values.

Argument 9: **Right-wing populism relies on inequality and is the political philosophy of society's losers. Since we'll always have inequality and losers in society, we'll always have right-wing populism (or, "The Tragic Society, Part 2").**

Refutation: In Chapters Two and Three, it was argued that those who are most drawn to right-wing populism in Ireland and Europe tend on average to be the less well-off, those whose marketable skills are weaker and who therefore perceive a keener threat from the entry into society of others. However, as in Argument 8 above, it would be bizarre to adopt a fatalistic attitude about populism on this basis. It is true that social inequality is a chronic and indeed intensifying aspect of human life between and within most societies (see Callinicos, 2000). But if anything, this provides yet another good reason to confront inequality and its consequences. It also highlights the importance of the guaranteed provision of basic social goods. Part of the unfortunate thrust of late capitalism is the threat to "privileged" workers of the advanced societies and the sustained efforts to restructure their conditions with increased contract labour and demands for flexibility. In this regard, we can see that Betz's (1994) analysis (outlined in Chapter Four; also see Argument 1 in this chapter) does capture some of the phenomenon often labelled as post-modernisation. The problem then is not equality but the greater concern about its permanence. The French sociologist Bourdieu has spoken of a new *precarité* or insecurity in people's lives:

> objective insecurity supports a generalised subjective insecurity which today affects, at the heart of an advanced economy, the majority of the workers and even those who are not or not yet directly hit. (1998: 99, quoted in Callinicos, 2000: 12)

This insecurity leads to a greater fear about the future and resentment of the needs of others. What Inglehart has called the "authoritarian reflex" is a response to severe insecurity and rapid change; "nativist reactions [are] often found among the more traditional and less secure strata in industrial societies, especially during times of stress . . . the reaction to change takes the form of a rejection of the new" (1997; 38). Right-wing populism is not a consequence of social equality or basic rights but of their perceived fragility.

Argument 10: **It is not the business of social scientists to concern themselves with taking sides on political issues; they should restrict themselves to describing trends. Thus, this short book should have been even shorter and stopped at the end of Chapter Four.**

Refutation: Such an objection represents a nice reversal of Marx's aphorism that philosophers have only interpreted the world; the point is to change it. The notion, though, that social science is never prescriptive is touchingly naïve; the reality is that social science, even when it doesn't intend it, is at least subtly prescriptive about "functional" or "dysfunctional" societies or social phenomena. Difficult social problems by their very nature attract more interest among those working in the human sciences and inevitably social scientists have personal views about those problems. Even when, for example, experimental psychologists have tried to be disinterested in the laboratory, they often inadvertently bias their findings according to their own expectations (see Gergen, 1973). Or when prominent US sociologists in an attempt to be "value-free" described a racist lynching in Texas as a "useful illustration of the function of mob action for the management of tension of some of its members" (Bredemeier and Stephenson, 1962: 161, note 19), do we think that they have found a satisfactory neutral position? Of course not. Apparent academic calm in the face of such an event already suggests a political commitment. Far better to be clear about one's biases and, here, the bias has been openly opposed to right-wing populism.

REPRISE

I have attempted to show above, through argument and counter-argument, that one should not be fatalistic about the rise of right-wing populism — there are no necessary reasons why it should become a force of substance in Irish politics. This is not a contradiction of the perspective outlined towards the end of Chapter Four — that right-wing populism is likely to make a breakthrough. In Ireland, some socio-economic conditions are in place which seem likely to provide ammunition to the political forces of populism. Similar conditions in other European states have provided fertile ground for such political forces and it would be optimistic to think that the same will not occur in Ireland. For example, Irish levels of wealth have increased rapidly along with greater expectations of state provision, despite opposition to taxation. Ireland has attracted greater numbers of asylum-seekers and immigrants. There is evidence, through surveys, focus groups, as well as anecdote and media reports, that opinion towards these newcomers, especially those of an ethnic minority background, is growing more hostile, particularly among those who feel their own socio-economic status is insecure. This widespread public hostility may take shape as a tangible political force, just as growing Euro-scepticism has done. There is also a recurring moral panic about crime and social control in Irish society (see for example, Vincent Browne's article in the *Irish Times*, 23 April 2003 — "The Great 'Crime Crisis' hype"). The historic equation of foreigner and disease was given a brief shot in the arm with the SARS epidemic, apparently originating in China. A comparable mental equation between Muslim and terrorist grows more deeply ingrained in our social perception. As noted above, it would be optimistic to think that xenophobia, hostility to asylum-seekers, suspicion of Brussels, an authoritarian approach to crime, and fear of the outsider as disease-carrier or terrorist will not be linked into a seductive political programme as it has elsewhere.

But optimism is not always wrong — nothing is inevitable, especially in politics, and countering right-wing populism is feasible. People *can* be irrational and self-centred about issues but are not always so. A humane approach, while reiterating the meagreness of the numbers of newcomers arriving from outside Ireland and indeed Europe and the harshness of so many lives elsewhere, does not have to be naïve about immigration. As Fintan O'Toole has pointed out (*Irish Times*, 28 January 2003; "Dodging the Issues of Immigration"), certain problems do arise as people seek to cope with new patterns of immigration; "clearly if you run a maternity hospital, there is a problem with large numbers of previously unknown women arriving on your doorstep in the very late stages of pregnancy. If you are running a local school in an area where immigration is concentrated, it is not easy to cope with large numbers of pupils who have trouble with the English language". He notes that there may also be new issues around public health, crime and national insecurity. These problems represent a challenge to society. However, as O'Toole argues, one of the consequences of racism "is that it pollutes the normal policy discourse that ought to surround any of these issues". Right-wing populism tends to contribute to the pollution of the debate and makes it more rather than less difficult to engage with these issues because of the climate it creates: a climate whereby open debate is undermined because people fear being labelled "racist" when they hold humane but non-consensus positions on certain questions. Established political forces can also play a role. As well as demanding more transparency at an EU level (see Argument 2 above), transparency is also needed at a national level and within both the asylum and immigration systems (although this hardly needs stating; one never hears demands for a "non-transparent" or an opaque system). For example, Dr Martin Ruhs (2003), a visiting research fellow, has suggested that the Irish Employment Visa system is best characterised as *"laissez-faire"* or essentially "unmanaged" in terms of the number entering, unlike, say, similar schemes run in Singapore and Hong Kong. A stronger criticism was made by the National Consultative Committee on Racism and Interculturalism (NCCRI) who have called for a move away from what they label "an *ad hoc* reactionary approach to migration and towards a planned and managed strategy" (quoted in *The Irish Times*, 22 April 2003, p. 5). Consideration perhaps could be given to a permanent work visa programme with citizenship offered following a number of years of working in a country. Inevitably, states using these programme tend to award permanent visas to the very well educated, something that will not necessarily aid the very many from elsewhere willing to take jobs demanding low skills. While a lottery for a small number of places might be agreed, one must be cautious about generating resentment through a perception that employers are seeking to use non-EU immigrants as the means of cheapening labour, undermining conditions for both native and foreign workers. Having a strong input by the trade union movement into the planning of a humane permanent visa system would seem sensible.

In terms of asylum, the Canadian system, which tries to be generous in its rules, might provide a good model. Partly this is because "it has a more generous definition of eligibility than most other countries" (*The Economist*, 15 March 2003, p. 36, special report on asylum). It also is more generous in its interpretation of its rules. For example, Canada and the UK in theory applied similar rules in dealing with Sri Lankan/Tamil asylum-seekers, yet Canada allowed 82 per cent of applications while the UK allowed 0.2 per cent (see Dummett, 2001: 37). Canada also does not use the full, expensive and cumbersome asylum system for those who are unlikely to be turned back (e.g. Iraqi Kurds under the Saddam regime, or indeed Ireland with the Kosovar refugees). The reality though for Ireland is that its common travel policy area with the UK makes it more likely that it, rather than Canada, will provide the model for dealing with issues of immigration and asylum.

A system that is transparent, bureaucratically efficient and fair *and* that is approved of by all may be an impossibility but at least where government is seen as trying to work towards building one, the resentment feeding into right-wing populist forces will be undermined. Furthermore, government, major organisations such as the churches and perhaps especially the media, have a role in continuing to make clear the increasing interdependence of all societies and peoples and must come down hard on those seeking to exploit sensitive issues for political gain. A comprehensive education system must highlight the historical reality that the flow of human traffic for so long was of Europeans *to* Africa, Asia and the Americas and make clear that current generations of both Irish and Europeans have responsibilities in turn. Massive bottlenecks in the provision of housing and medical care have the potential to create ugly rivalries between different groups experiencing need. If the state cannot improve on its efforts in these areas, or for ideological reasons is reluctant to push aside market provision when it fails the general public, then those with a populist message will obtain the upper hand.

REFERENCES

Allport, G.W. (1954), *The Nature of Prejudice*, Reading, MA: Addison-Wesley.

Angel, B. and Hjern, A. (1992), *Meeting Children of Refugees and their Families*, Lund: Studentlitteratur.

Arendt, H. (1951), *The Burden of Our Time* [Published also as *The Origins of Totalitarianism*], London: Secker & Warburg.

Batson, C.D. (1995), "Prosocial motivation: Why do we help others?" in A. Tesser (ed.), *Advanced Social Psychology*, London: McGraw-Hill.

Beevor, A. (2001), *Berlin: The Downfall 1945*, London: Viking.

Bergmann, W. and Erb, R. (1986), "Kommunikationslatenz, moral und offentliche meining", *Kolner Zeitschrift für Soziologie und Sozialpsychologie*, Vol. 38, pp. 223–46.

Betz, H.G. (1994), *Radical Right-Wing Populism in Western Europe*, New York: St Martin's Press.

Bogardus, E.S. (1933), "A social distance scale", *Sociology and Social Research*, Vol. 17, pp. 265–71.

Bourdieu, P. (1998), *Contre-Feux*, Paris: Liber, Raisons d'Agir.

Bredemeier, H.C. and Stephenson, R.M. (1962), *The Analysis of Social Systems*, New York: Holt, Rinehart and Winston.

Callinicos, A. (2000), *Equality*, Cambridge: Polity Press.

Carroll, S. (2003), *Anti-Racism Ideology: Multicultural and Colour-Blind Perspectives*, unpublished thesis, Dublin: Department of Psychology, University College Dublin.

Casey, S. and O'Connell, M. (2000), "Pain and Prejudice: Assessing the Experience of Racism in Ireland" in M. MacLachlan and M. O'Connell (eds.), *Cultivating Pluralism: Psychological, Social and Cultural Perspectives on a Changing Ireland*, Dublin: Oak Tree Press.

Castles, S., Crawley, H. and Loghna, S. (2003), *States of Fear: Causes and Patterns of Forced Migration to the EU and Policy Responses* (IPPR report), London: Central Books.

Curry, P. (2000), "'She never let them in . . .': Popular Reactions to Refugees Arriving in Dublin" in M. MacLachlan and M. O'Connell (eds.), *Cultivating Pluralism: Psychological, Social and Cultural Perspectives on a Changing Ireland*, Dublin: Oak Tree Press.

Curtis, L. (1984), *Nothing But the Same Old Story: The Roots of Anti-Irish Racism*, London: Information on Ireland.

Dummett, M. (2001), *On Immigration and Refugees*, London: Routledge.

The Economist (various issues), London.

Essed, P. (1984), *Alledaags Racisme*, Amsterdam: Sara.

Eurobarometer 47.1 (1997), *Archive study number 2936*, European Commission: DGV, Luxembourg and Brussels.

Eurobarometer 57.1 (2002), *Archive study number 3639*, European Commission: DGV, Luxembourg and Brussels.

Eurobarometer 1970–1999 (2001), *The Mannheim Trend File*, European Commission: DGV, Luxembourg and Brussels.

Eurostat (2003), "Social Protection in Europe" (by G. Abramovici), *Statistics in Focus*, Theme 3 — 3/2003, Luxembourg and Brussels: European Commission.

Fanning, B. (2002), *Racism and Social Change in the Republic of Ireland*, Manchester: Manchester University Press.

FitzGerald, G. (2002), *Reflections on the Irish State*, Dublin: Irish Academic Press.

Freriks, P. (1990), *Franse Anti-Racisten Willen Handen Vuil Maken*, De Volkskrant, 1 May 1990, p. 2.

Friedman, M. (1998), Interview available on the web, www.hoover. stanford.edu/publications/digest/982/friedman3.html.

Gaertner, S.L. and Dovidio, J.F. (1986), "The Aversive Form of Racism" in J.F. Dovidio and S.L. Gaertner (eds.), *Prejudice, Discrimination, and Racism: Theory and Research*, New York: Academic Press.

Gergen, K.J. (1973), "Social Psychology as History", *Journal of Personality and Social Psychology*, Vol. 26, pp. 309–20.

Gurr, T.R. (1970), *Why Men Rebel*, Princeton, NJ: Princeton University Press.

Hayter, T. (2000), *Open Borders: The Case against Immigration Controls*, London: Pluto Press.

Hewstone, M. and Brown, R.J. (1986), "Contact Is Not Enough: An Intergroup Perspective on the Contact Hypothesis" in M. Hewstone and R. Brown (eds.), *Contact and Conflict in Intergroup Encounters*, Oxford: Basil Blackwell.

Hobbes, T. (1651/1904), *Leviathan*, Cambridge: Cambridge University Press.

Hogg, M.A. and Vaughan, G.M. (2002), *Social Psychology* (3rd ed.), Harlow: Prentice Hall (Pearson Education).

Hood, R. (1992), *Race and Sentencing*, Oxford: Clarendon Press.

Howard, J.W. and Rothbart, M. (1980), "Social Categorization and Memory for Ingroup and Outgroup Behavior", *Journal of Personality and Social Psychology*, Vol. 38, pp. 301–10.

Hutton, W. (2002), *The World We're In*, London: Little Brown.

ISPAS Survey (2002) (For survey details, see "Introduction" in D. Payne, J. Garry, and N. Hardiman, (forthcoming), *Changing Irish Values*, Dublin: The Liffey Press.

Jackman, M. and Muha, M.J. (1984), "Education and Intergroup Attitudes: Moral Enlightenment, Superficial Democratic Commitment or Ideological Refinement?", *American Sociological Review*, Vol. 49; pp. 751–69.

Kennedy, F., Sinnott, R., Marsh, M. and Garry, J. (forthcoming) "Irish Social and Political Cleavages" in D. Payne, J. Garry, and N. Hardiman (forthcoming), *Changing Irish Values*, Dublin: The Liffey Press.

Kovel, J. (1970), *White Racism: A Psychohistory*, New York: Pantheon.

Layte, R., Maître, B., Nolan, B., Watson, D., Whelan, C.T., Williams, J. and Casey, B. (2001), *Monitoring Poverty Trends and Exploring Poverty Dynamics in Ireland*, Policy Research Series (PRS) No. 41, Dublin: Economic and Social Research Institute.

Lee, J. (1989), *Ireland 1912–1985: Politics and Society*, Cambridge: Cambridge University Press.

Lukes, S. (1974), *Power: A Radical View*, London: Macmillan.

Lipset, S.M. (1981), *Political Man* (2nd ed.), Baltimore: John Hopkins University Press.

McConahay, J.B. (1983), "Modern Racism and Modern Discrimination: The Effects of Race, Racial Attitudes and Context on Simulated Hiring Decisions", *Personality and Social Psychology Bulletin*, Vol. 9, pp. 551–8.

McConahay, J.B. (1986), "Modern Racism, Ambivalence, and the Modern Racism Scale" in J. Dovidio and S. Gaertner (eds.), *Prejudice, Discrimination, and Racism*, New York: Academic Press.

MacGréil, M. (1996), *Prejudice in Ireland Revisited*, Dublin: Survey and Research Unit, Maynooth.

McVeigh, R. and Lentin, R. (2002), "Situated Racisms: A Theoretical Introduction" in R. Lentin and R. McVeigh (eds.), *Racism and Anti-Racism in Ireland*, Belfast: Beyond the Pale Publications.

Martens, P.L. (1995), "Immigrants and Crime Prevention" in P.H. Wikström, R.V. Clarke and J. McCord (eds.), *Integrating Crime Prevention Strategies: Propensity and Opportunity*, Stockholm: Fritzes.

Martens, P.L. (1997), "Immigrants, Crime and Criminal Justice in Sweden" in M. Tonry (ed.), *Ethnicity, Crime and Immigration: Comparative and Cross-National Perspectives*, Chicago: University of Chicago Press.

Nagel, T. (1991), *Equality and Partiality*, Oxford: Oxford University Press.

National Consultative Committee on Racism and Interculturalism; website at www.nccri.com.

OECD (2001), *Labour Force Statistics: 1980–2000*, Paris: OECD.

OECD (2003), *Main Economic Indicators* (March), Paris, OECD.

Office of the Refugee Applications Commissioner (2002), *Annual Report 2001*, Dublin, Office of the Refugee Applications Commissioner.

Patton, D. (1997), Book review of H.G. Betz's *Radical Right-Wing Populism in Western Europe*, in *Stanford Electronic Humanities Review*, Vol. 5.2, pp. 1–3.

Payne, D., J. Garry, and N. Hardiman (forthcoming), *Changing Irish Values*, Dublin: The Liffey Press.

Pearson, G. (1983), *Hooligan: A History of Respectable Fears*, London: Macmillan.

Pettigrew, T.F. (1997), "Generalized Intergroup Contact Effects on Prejudice", *Personality and Social Psychology Bulletin*, Vol. 23; pp. 173–85.

Pettigrew, T.F. and Meertens, R.W. (1995), "Subtle and Blatant Prejudice in Western Europe", *European Journal of Social Psychology*, Vol. 25, pp. 57–75.

Pinker, S. (2002), *The Blank Slate: The Modern Denial of Human Nature*, London: Allen Lane (Penguin).

Pitman, R.K., Shalev, A.Y. and Orr, S.P. (2000), "Posttraumatic Stress Disorder: Emotion, Conditioning, and Memory" in M.S. Gazzaniga (ed.), *The New Cognitive Neurosciences* (2nd ed.), Cambridge, MA: MIT Press.

Quinley, H.E. and Glock, C.Y. (1979), *Anti-Semitism in America*, New York: Free Press.

Ringen, S. (2003), "Population Crisis in Europe", *Times Literary Supplement*, 3 March.

The Rough Guide to Ireland (1993), London: Rough Guides (Penguin).

Ruhs, M. (2003), *Managing the Employment of Non-EU Nationals in Ireland*, "Work-in-Progress" Seminar given at The Policy Institute at Trinity College Dublin, 8 April.

Sears, D.D. (1988), "Symbolic Racism" in P.A. Katz and D.A. Taylor (eds.), *Eliminating Racism: Profiles in Controversy*, New York: Plenum.

Sherif, M. (1966), *Group Conflict and Co-operation: Their Social Psychology*, London: Routledge & Kegan Paul.

Sinnott, R. (1995), *Irish Voters Decide*, Manchester: Manchester University Press.

Smith, A. (1759/1976), *The Theory of Moral Sentiments*, Indianapolis: Liberty Classics.

Smith, J.P. and Edmonston, B. (eds.) (1997), *The New Americans: Economic, Demographic and Fiscal Effects of Immigration*, Washington: National Research Council.

Sowell, T. (1987), *A Conflict of Visions: Ideological Origins of Political Struggles*, New York: Quill.

Tajfel, H. (1981), *Human Groups and Social Categories*, Cambridge: Cambridge University Press.

Time Out Guide Dublin (3rd ed) (2002), London: Penguin.

Tonry, M. (1997), "Ethnicity, Crime and Immigration" in M. Tonry (ed.), *Ethnicity, Crime and Immigration: Comparative and Cross-National Perspectives*, Chicago: University of Chicago Press.

Tournier, P. (1999), *Statistique Pénale Annuelle du Conseil de l'Europe, Enquête 1997*, Strasbourg: Conseil de l'Europe.

UNHCR (2002), *Statistical Yearbook 2001*.

US Committee for Refugees; website at www.refugees.org.

Wacquant, L. (1999), "Suitable Enemies: Foreigners and Immigrants in the Prisons of Europe", *Punishment and Society*, Vol. 1, pp. 215–22.

Zellman, G.L. and Sears, D.O. (1971), "Childhood Origins of Tolerance for Dissent", *Journal of Social Issues*, Vol. 27, pp. 109–36.

INDEX

The Count's Cats

Inscribed for Eleanor and Madeline

by

Jeremy Mallinson

In the hope that you will enjoy their narrative for Cats are great and fun.

Llumina Press

With all best wishes for the future

Jeremy Mallinson

By the same author

Okavango Adventure
Earning Your Living with Animals
Modern Classic Animal Stories (Editor)
The Shadow of Extinction
The Facts About a Zoo
Travels in Search of Endangered Species
" Durrelliania" - An Illustrated Checklist

Illustrations by Dixie-Lee Whiteman

Requests for permission to make copies of any part of this work should be mailed to Permissions Department, Llumina Press, PO Box 772246, Coral Springs, FL 33077-2246
ISBN: 1-9323560-81-5

Printed in the United States of America by Llumina Press